Choosing Dance Over Despair

How I Found Keys to Joy and Recovery While Living with Serious Mental Illness

Margalea Warner

Contents

Cover design by Danijela Mijailovic

Book Production and Publishing Services by Miramare Ponte Press
www.miramarepontepress.com

Hardback ISBN-13: 979-8-9986380-1-5
Paperback ISBN-13: 979-8-9986380-2-2
eBook ISBN-13: 979-8-9986380-0-8

Library of Congress Control Number: 2025907360

Chapter 1

Looking Beyond the Locked Door

This memoir celebrates a faith journey of recovery from serious mental illness, using dance as a metaphor for rebuilding my life by choosing joy and gratitude even at times that seem hopeless and overwhelming. My hope is that through my story, others will feel inspired to believe there's hope in living with mental illness, both for the individual and their loved ones.

In the literal act of dancing, I'm challenged. Once, my seventh-grade PE teacher videotaped us girls square dancing and replayed it to us, saying, "This is where Margalea messed up and set everyone else off course."

My balance is not the greatest. As a teenager, I stayed overnight at the home of my best friend, Martha. She offered to sleep on the top bunk, but I assured her I would be fine. We said goodnight. I was dreaming that I was crossing a busy street, and my legs must have started running in my sleep because I tumbled right out of bed. No harm done. However clumsy I am in my sleep, I *do* have the grace to laugh at myself. It became a favorite story of Martha's children, who repeatedly ask her to tell about the time when Aunt Margalea fell out of bed.

I have since learned that dancing, like many things that give us joy, doesn't have to be perfect to be worth trying. I finally learned to square dance with my French-Canadian date as a college student at Laval University in Quebec City. I wish that PE teacher could have seen how well I followed the caller's shout: *Swingez votre partneur.*

Another dance-like thing that I started out hilariously bad at was tai chi. When my elbows were supposed to be down, they stuck out like I was doing the chicken dance. I was never sure if I was doing *brush knee and twist step left* or *brush knee and twist step right.* But I kept at it, resisting my inner PE teacher saying, *"You're never going to get good at this. So quit trying."*

I didn't quit—I got better at it! Twelve years later, I'm still practicing. My teacher calls me the Triumphant Tai Chi Tortoise for my slow but steady persistence.

The Bible uses the image of dancing as an expression of joy and gratitude. Jeremiah 31:4 says,

> *"I will build you up again, and you, Virgin Is-*
> *rael, will be rebuilt. Again, you will take*
> *up your timbrels and go out to dance with*
> *the joyful."*

I have lived with serious mental illness since my early twenties and am now in my mid-sixties. My mental health condition was not caused by personal weakness, lack of character, or poor upbringing. I get to choose how to respond to my mental health challenges and, over a lifetime, now make better choices.

Just like learning to square dance or tai chi, it took practice to choose dance over despair. I previously chose despair to the point of attempting to take my life multiple times. Traumatic events challenged me, and I had to process them to move on. Sometimes I felt numb and frozen.

I finally realized that my thinking was off-key and accepted piano tuning for the mind in the form of medicine and cognitive psychotherapy. I committed to taking my medicine consistently. I got stronger in my spiritual strength by reciting Psalm 118:24:

> *"The Lord has done it this very day; let us*
> *rejoice today and be glad."*

I now live in recovery, not cure. Right now, there is no medical cure for most mental illnesses, although better treatments are being researched, and I have benefited from some of them. In my experience, God has used doctors and medicine to heal me, but there is more to the wholeness of life than medical treatment.

I've been free of hospitalizations for almost three decades. There's no shame in being hospitalized when you're in a mental health crisis, but thriving in your community year after year is something to celebrate. As the years of freedom added up like pennies in a piggy bank, I began celebrating anniversaries by adding actual keys to a shadowbox that I labeled with concepts that had helped me get better.

To me, dance is any movement of body or spirit that renews joy, love, and gratitude. People of all ages are invited to join in the dance. Jeremiah 31:13 says,

> *"Then young women will dance and be glad,*
> *young men and old as well. I will turn*
> *their mourning into gladness; I will give*
> *them comfort and joy instead of sorrow."*

I choose to dance in celebration of a life that God and I are rebuilding together. I don't want to plod along joylessly, head bent, missing out on all the beauty I can see if I just look up. I choose to dance, accepting the invitation to dance with God and God's purposes.

While I'm not a ballerina, the way I lived in recovery from serious mental illness inspired a ballet! The ballet is called *Unfinished* and was performed at the University of Iowa in 2022.

This book entitles you to a front-row seat to that performance.

Even if you don't have a diagnosed mental illness or don't know anyone who does, our hearts are all in need of mending from something. Why don't I tell you my story, and you can decide what recovery means to you. Maybe some of my keys will open your locked doors, or maybe you'll be inspired to create your own keys. Let's see what might be behind some of those locked doors.

The heaviness of my sigh matched the weight of the steel door that locked behind me with a loud clunk. I hadn't committed a crime, and I wasn't in jail. I was in a locked hospital psychiatric ward because I had a no-fault brain disorder called schizophrenia.

The hospital wasn't a terrible place to be. Unlike the hellish, insane asylums of half a century ago, patients are treated with respect and dignity. The awful practice of lobotomy has long since been discarded. This hospital was renowned for evidence-based medical treatment. There was a sunny Day Room where smoking wasn't allowed. Eating with other patients in the dining room helped things feel a little more normal.

Except I didn't want to be here. Again. For the past fifteen years, I had been in and out of the hospital as if I were stuck in a revolving door. Seeing nursing staff walking around with a hefty set of keys on their belts made me envious.

I wanted the key to my apartment where I lived with my pets. I wanted the key to my mailbox, where I hoped an acceptance letter for my writing awaited. A lifelong non-driver, I didn't want car keys, but I wanted the key to my bicycle lock so I could go on a spin around the neighborhood. There had been other times when I was discharged from the hospital too soon, and I ended up sicker, but this time, I thought I was ready to take charge of my wellness. I wanted back the life these hospitalizations were interrupting.

I told you schizophrenia is a no-fault brain disease, and that is true. But the reason I was on a locked psych floor was that the doctors didn't trust me to resist the temptation to take my life. Sometimes, I didn't trust myself to find a reason to go on living either. I confess and lament that I have risked, over and over, doing something that would completely interrupt my life, a life that I believe God has a plan and a purpose for. Now, I was pledging to risk living instead of dying.

The door to the unit had a small window with wire mesh. All you could see through it was a short hallway blocked by another locked door. If only I could have seen through this door and all the doors locked behind me in an endless tunnel. Even in the darkest times, I'd stayed curious, ready to be surprised by the next turn in the winding road I was traveling.

If only I could have looked beyond these doors into the future. What if I placed an imaginary bookmark on June 9, 1995, and scribbled on the current page of my life's book, "Last Psychiatric Hospitalization." Then, I let angels turn the pages with their wing feathers until we land on November 11, 2022, Hancher Auditorium, Iowa City, Iowa. This was a theater that had been destroyed in the floods of 2008 and rebuilt on higher ground. And my life, as of this night, was also rebuilt on higher ground.

I looked at the program I was holding, seeing a photo of a young dancer in a simple white dress leaping with her arms outstretched as if she were flying. In gold letters were the words, *"In Motion, Dance*

Gala 2022." I turned the pages of the program to Act 1, Dance 2 *UNFINISHED*. I would have been amazed by the words at the bottom of the page: *Inspiration: Margalea Warner and Michael Judge.*

I held my breath with excitement as the spotlight shone on a young woman in a simple white dress walking across the stage while making slow, meditative tai chi movements. I heard the opening chords of Schubert's unfinished symphony. I marveled at huge shining keys above the dancer and the dancers who joined her on the stage. I witnessed a dance of courage. A dance of disturbing truth. A dance of strange beauty. A dance of vulnerable self-revealing. A dance of a tortoise's persistence outdistancing the hare. A dance that was interrupted, as were the lives it celebrated. A dance that, though unfinished, ended with hope.

I would have known that I had keys to open one locked door after another. I would have known that I would be forgiven, healed, and renewed. I would have heard an invitation to choose dance over despair.

Postscript: You can watch a video of ballet at this link on my web page. It's about 16 minutes.

https://margalea.com/2022/11/14/unfinished

Chapter 2

Warning Signs and the Key of Family Love

I was the well-loved child of parents who welcomed me into the world as a big surprise when my mother was 39 and my father was 44. It was a second marriage for both of them and they weren't anticipating having a child. My mother had a son by her previous husband. My half-brother David was 14 years older than I was. I didn't grow up with him, so I was like an only child. An important family member was my cat, Who Me, who got her name for her innocent demeanor when caught in mischief, as if she was asking, "Who, me?"

I was a creative child. My mother wrote down some of the stories I told her about elves and fairies. Evidence of my early writing were the words "once upon a time" engraved into the wood of our family dining room table because I pressed down so hard with a fat pencil. I had to help sand and refinish the table, my first experience with editing. I loved drawing crayon cards. My dad saved one I gave him on Father's Day, saying, "You are the bestest daddy in the world." I even found a cardboard bookmark I made for my mother when I was going through her things after she died. That's interesting because I still make bookmarks.

My father sent a poem I wrote to Wee Wisdom Magazine, and they published it. It went like this: Who Me is a cat/and not a rat/and that is that.

Despite my loving family, I was sad and lonely at times. I tended to have more grown-up friends than children my own age. My parents sent me to private school from kindergarten through third grade. I got a grounding in reading and writing because of this. In third grade, my teacher was harsh and spanked children with a paddle in front of the whole class. I was so frightened of her, I never spoke above a whisper. I made friends with a boy named Jamie in my class who was one of her victims. I let him know I thought she was mean and that he didn't deserve it. I have a snapshot of the two of us holding hands, me wearing a ballet tutu that my mother had made for me. The photo later became a reminder to choose dance over despair.

In fourth grade, I went to public school. Unfortunately, this teacher wasn't much kinder than the third-grade teacher. She didn't hit her students physically, but she slapped us with shaming words. I had just gotten eyeglasses the summer before, and I would conveniently forget to wear them to school, so I couldn't read the board but could still read the storybooks I brought from home. Once I "woke up" from my book to realize the other children had gone off to recess and I was alone in the classroom. When I did go to the playground, the other children wouldn't play with me. I remember sliding down a grassy hill instead of the slide. I still didn't speak very loudly, so the teacher sent me to a speech therapist. The speech therapist was friendly and kind and I talked very clearly with her about my sister, the cat. She didn't think there was anything wrong with me.

When I was in fifth grade, we moved to the Maryland suburbs to be closer to my dad's workplace, Miles Glass Company. My fifth-grade teacher, Mr. MacIntosh, changed my young life for the better. He protected me from bullies. He encouraged my writing. He took us on a class field trip weekend to Colonial Williamsburg. I think it is because of him that I had the courage to be a writer. He proved to me that I had something to say that other people would want to hear.

Sixth grade was the year my parents' marriage started unraveling. Mom quit her job as a graphic artist, saying she wanted to stay home with me. We couldn't afford house payments on the Maryland house without her income. We moved to an apartment, one of the few we could find that allowed cats, so I could keep Who Me. One of the losses to my father was that he couldn't keep his rose garden, which included bushes he transplanted from his father's garden. It made me so sad for him. At the time, I was reading C.S. Lewis' Narnia chronicles. In *The Last Battle,* the children get catapulted back to Narnia by dying in a train accident. I had the dangerous idea that if I died, I could get to Narnia, too. I really wanted to see Aslan and pet his mane.

I went on a children's retreat at Church of the Saviour Dayspring Retreat Farm with my youth group leader, who became concerned because I was so quiet and sad. He told my parents he was afraid I was suicidal. I bristled and told them that I was not. I didn't want to kill myself; I just wanted to shift into a fantasy world where I would be free from my parents' conflict.

When I was 13, my mother left my father, taking me with her to live in an apartment in Kensington, Maryland, where cats were allowed. Who Me was also about 13 years old. My mother went back to work full-time, and I came home from school in the afternoon to an empty apartment. Because I kept losing the apartment key, Mom got me a necklace to wear it around my neck. I felt pretty wearing it and somehow it made me feel more grown up. So began my love of keys! My chores when I got home were to feed Who Me and then play with her, dangling her mouse on a string toy. Later, we got the cat a collar and a leash and I would take her on walks. I even let her climb small trees with it on. I have a picture of her perched on a low branch of a flowering tree, looking regal.

Because we moved in October, I changed junior high schools in the middle of my seventh-grade school year. The first day there, I wore glasses with green frames, but that afternoon we went to the optical shop to pick up a new prescription of glasses with red frames. The other kids noticed and commented on it. I don't think they were trying to be mean or tease me, but I didn't know what to say and I decided to just ignore them, hoping they would stop. That backfired because they called me stuck up and really *did* tease me.

Girls in my home economics class teased me about not wearing a bra. They asked me if I was a fighter. I told them I only fought cats, thinking, of course, of Who Me. That made them bully me even more. Every day when the last school bell rang, I ran the six blocks home, though I never actually saw anyone chasing me. I found refuge in my friendship with two girls, Martha Foster and Mary Rittenhouse, who let me sit with them at lunch and did things after school with me. We had in common that our first names all started with MAR, and as Mary pointed out later, that made us marvelous friends. We continue to be in touch over 50 years later.

My father remained a faithful and loving father. We got together on Wednesday afternoons and went on what we joked were "cheap dates": walking to the public library or to free concerts in the park, eating at McDonald's or packing a picnic lunch. On Sundays, he took me to worship and Sunday School at Church of the Saviour in Washington, D.C. We especially liked listening to classical music on the radio. Sometimes, we would sing in the car, too. To celebrate my thirteenth birthday, he took me to Vermont to visit the Warner property.

I continued to long for an escape, less now about getting to Narnia and more about being delivered from meanness. I fantasized about my funeral and how all the kids who bullied me would hate themselves for it. I also dreamed that my journals would be found and published like *The Diary of Anne Frank*. Like Tom Sawyer watching his funeral while very much alive, I found comfort by imagining myself listening in on my own memorial service.

But there were still bright spots in my teenage years. My father mailed me typed letters several times a week. My mom kept maps of the whole area in her glove compartment and we would go on "adventure" rides discovering new places. We would stop at McDonald's for French fries and toss a few of them out the car window for the sparrows to snatch up. Who Me, who had become a senior cat and was on a diet of chicken baby food, slept right beside my pillow at night.

Psalm 68:6 says, "*God sets the lonely in families.*" It was a protective factor to have a family that loved me unconditionally. I do not blame my family for the mental illness that gradually evolved, something I think was present in my brain at birth. As I have gotten to know the family members of my peers with mental illness, I've grown in empathy and understanding for their struggle to support and protect their family members. It's true that I have known individuals with mental illness who truly did come through the trauma of abusive family life. But this was not the case for me. I think most families do the best they can. Families and individuals can both do better when they are educated about mental illness and are given hope for recovery.

Though there were warning signs of a furious brainstorm ahead, my parents sheltered me, anchored me, and got me through my teens. I was rooted in love and was able to mature and overcome obstacles because of it.

Chapter 3

My Brother and the Key of a Renewed Right Spirit

I said in the last chapter that I did not grow up with my half-brother, David Kingsley Crombie. But to say he was only a half-brother would be a half-truth and a whole lie.

I have a vivid memory of shouting out my bedroom window to my neighbor Margaret Jones, "I have a brother and he's coming to live with us."

Margaret shouted back, "You do not!"

"Do too!" I shouted.

"Do not!" she shouted. I had to admit, it sounded like a tall tale.

At the time, I was five years old and my brother was 19. When I was just a young child, my grandparents took him with them to California where my grandfather was taking a position as a physics professor. It was a challenging time for my family; I have to give you the backstory:

My mother, Eleanor Louise Brown, met my father, Philip Charles Warner, responding to his ad in the paper that he wanted to share some old copies of Guideposts magazine. They found out they had more than their faith in common: they were both single after divorces, they both grew up in Arlington, Virginia, and they made each other laugh. My mother's brother, who died as a toddler, was named Philip, so she had tender feelings for that name. Their friendship blossomed into love. They claimed Isaiah 35:1 as the verse that captured how their relationship brought surprising joy in the desert of loneliness after their divorces:

> "The desert and the parched land will be
>   glad; the wilderness will rejoice and
>   blossom."

My father proposed and my mother accepted.

But my father didn't propose to my brother, and David most certainly didn't say yes. When my mother married my father, my brother, about 13 years old, was used to having Mom to himself. Mom and David had a comfortable routine in their apartment, with certain days of the week for grocery shopping and house cleaning, other days for going to the park, and nights for watching the *I Remember Mama* show on television. After the marriage, they were a household of three, and the friction was sharp, even more so when I was born and needed so much love and attention. My grandparents stepped in and took my brother with them to California. It was a hard separation for my mom and brother, and I think it broke their hearts.

Now, 13 years later, my brother was 19 and wanted to return to Arlington, Virginia, and stay with us. Mom said yes and prepared a room in our attic for him. I was so excited to meet him.

While he wasn't around much in my early life, he didn't hate me or forget about me while he was away. I have a picture of me as a toddler wearing a red Chinese silk jacket and pants he had sent me as a birthday present. And years later, he told me that after I was born, before he left for California, he helped plant a tree in my honor that he would water with partially melted ice from the ice box where we had milk delivered to our door. I witnessed that tree grow to over six feet tall. That doesn't sound like something he would do if he hated me.

We went to the bus station to pick him up. I remember thinking how handsome he was. He had curly brown hair and neatly trimmed side-burns. He was wearing jeans and a blue plaid shirt that accented his blue eyes. He gave Mom a hug but was rather stiff toward my dad. He bent down to my eye level and ruffled my hair with his hand. I thought, *Boy, is Margaret Jones going to be surprised that I DO have a brother, and he's pretty cool.*

My thinking is fuzzy about the months that followed. His friendliness wore off. I wasn't allowed in the attic where he slept, and that's where he spent most of his time. He would slam doors in ways that scared me. He even got to the point where he would walk around me as if I weren't there. I wondered what I could have done to make him reject me.

My mother explained it to me years later. She said that my brother had inherited the propensity to alcoholism from his father. She had left his father, David Crombie, when David was a baby because "he was spending all the money on booze and there wasn't anything left for me and the baby." David never knew his father. But somehow, like his father, he drank to excess and it created chaos in his behavior. He tried drinking vodka, thinking Mom wouldn't smell it on his breath. But Mom wasn't fooled. She threw him out of the house after just a few months.

At bedtime, when I said my prayers, Mom would have me pray from Psalm 51:10, *"Renew a right spirit within me."* I added, "Also, renew a right spirit within my brother David." Kind of appropriate since that is one of the psalms of King David, huh?

Then a miracle happened. David found help from Alcoholics Anonymous. He accepted that he was powerless over alcohol. He reached out to his higher power. He had an AA sponsor who helped him find his way into sober living. My mother was so proud of him! He was still a deeply wounded person and wasn't always an easy sibling to live with. But he was on the road to healing and our family with him.

Christmas morning in 1969, when I was ten and we were living in a new house in Maryland, David joined our family for the holiday. Even our cat, Who Me, had a Christmas present. It was a cardboard house with holes in it that you could poke a feather on a stick inside to tease her to play in it. She loved it! My brother and I couldn't stop giggling at her playful antics. Somehow, the dam was broken, and we started talking and being friends again. There was a big snowstorm that day and we went sledding down the hill in front of the house.

There's more to the story about me and my brother and how God gave us both keys to freedom. But for now, it's enough to know we were brother and sister on a journey to wholeness.

Chapter 4

The Key of Compeer Friendship

Going 250 miles away from my home in Kensington, Maryland, to start college in Bethany, West Virginia, was both exhilarating and terrifying. I chose Bethany College because it was a small liberal arts school where I hoped I could make friends and become a writer. Even at 18, I knew I wanted to be the kind of writer who would draw in my readers and make them laugh and cry with me. Neither of my parents had a college degree. It wasn't that they weren't smart, talented, hardworking people, but their life circumstances just didn't include that possibility. My father attended the Washington School for Secretaries and then enlisted in the Navy during World War II. He was promoted to be secretary to the captain of the aircraft carrier he was on in the South Pacific. My mother studied dress design in New York City and went on to be a draftsman and a graphic artist.

I had my heart set on going to college ever since I was a young child. My parents opened a savings account for me when I was six years old. They were proud of me for doing well in high school and wanted me to follow my dreams, but it took courage for them to let me go. The expense was considerable, and we were not a wealthy family. I did get loans and scholarships and earned money during the summer doing secretarial work. I had never been that far from home before. I'm so grateful they let me take that chance, which included the possibility that I could fail.

Not only did I leave my parents, but I left my feline sister, Who Me. Mom said that she left one of my dresser drawers open with a sweater that had my scent on it so Who Me could sleep there. Mom was a night owl and would sit and read late into the night. Who Me was used to my going to bed much earlier. About nine o'clock in the evening, she would walk into the living room and meow until Mom would get up and carry her to the dresser. By this time, Who Me was 18 years old, same as I was, except in cat years quite a bit older. We missed each other terribly.

One of my first semester classes was a small honors English class taught by Dr. Helen Louise McGuffie. For the first class, she invited us to come to her home, which was on a gravel road just outside of campus. I'm sure she gave us some sort of directions to get there, but I must have gotten them muddled because I found myself on a hot, dusty road with no house in sight. A young man with a dark tan was passing by, driving a farm tractor. When I asked him directions, he told me to hop on the back of his tractor and he would take me there. He got me there when the class was almost over. Dr. McGuffie got a glimpse of me through the window getting down off the tractor. She was not amused. And she wasn't pleased with the first writing assignment I submitted because the paper was torn from a spiral notebook with ragged edges. She believed that neatness counted. I procrastinated on writing papers until I had to do all-nighters. I was beginning to doubt my ability to be a writer.

But one thing I have to give Professor McGuffie credit for was that she introduced me to the amazing world of dictionaries. She had us look up the roots of words. She told us to go look at the many volumes of the Oxford English dictionary in the college library. I discovered a marvelous word in the dictionary: compeer. Compeer is a noun meaning one who is the peer or equal of another and also a companion or friend. It's from Old French, "*compere*," an appellation of friendly greeting, "friend, brother."

The compeer friendship of other students at Bethany helped me find the courage and confidence to continue toward my goals. There was Chris (short for Christine), who sat next to me in the back row of the lecture hall. We whispered and wrote notes to each other on the soles of our running shoes. We joked that they were footnotes. There was Beth, who would walk down the street singing, in a jazzy, spirited way, songs like, "Let the words of my mouth and the meditation of my heart be accepted in thy sight, O Lord, my rock and my redeeeeeeeemer." There were international students like Joo Chiang Lee from Malaysia and Tim Kabugi from Kenya.

The spring of my freshman year, I joined Pi Beta Phi sorority and chose Peggy as my big sister. The positive side of being in a sorority was that I had a real sense of belonging, even though I remained close to my friends who pledged GDI (Gol 'Darn Independent). The negative side was that there was a lot of alcohol abuse. It led to risky behavior. I remember asking one of the sorority sisters, "What happened to me last night?"

She said, "You were partying in your panties."

I'm so grateful I survived and went on to make better choices. Science backs the concept that human brains don't mature until we are in our mid to late twenties, so I try to give myself grace about it.

If I could go back in time to talk to my college-aged self, I would tell her, "Remember your why! You came to college to be a writer, not a drunk. This lifestyle isn't going to help you reach your goals.

Remember your brother David and his battle with alcoholism. Return to the prayer your mother taught you, 'Renew a right spirit within me.' You've got this because God's got you."

In the spring of 1978, a phone call from home saying Who Me had finally passed on set me reeling. I took some comfort knowing David had placed her body in a small suitcase and buried her in the park. But I felt I had betrayed her by going off to college and leaving her behind. By this time, she and I were 18 years old. No one understood me better than Who Me. I imagined reuniting with her if I took my life. I stopped going to the cafeteria for meals with my friends. I stayed in my dorm room instead, but I couldn't sleep. I started to give away possessions, like my cherished book on massage therapy, which I gave to my friend Chris.

My developing brain had a kind of brain attack. I saw a poster in the Student Health clinic saying not to take too much aspirin because it could be fatal. I stole a bottle of Bufferin from my roommate's closet, where she kept it for relief from hangovers. It was almost full. I took it and a bottle of water with me on a hiking trail on campus that led to a small waterfall. I swallowed every last pill, handful by handful, washing the bitter, salty tablets down with sips of water.

Something made me walk back to the sorority house and find Peggy, my big sister. I asked her if I could take a nap in her room because my dorm was noisy and it was giving me a headache. She knew intuitively that something more was wrong with me. She tucked me into bed at about three in the afternoon, but she stayed close by. Eventually, I started vomiting and having convulsions. Peggy demanded to know what kind of poison I had taken. I confessed to taking the aspirin. She called 911.

In Bethany, the first responders were all volunteers, mostly students and hospital staff. They were all close by and came immediately. They took me to the nearest hospital in Wheeling, West Virginia.

One of the student paramedics asked me why I had taken the aspirin. I told him I had a really bad headache. Talk about an understatement! The truth was that my brain hurt, my heart hurt, my whole self hurt.

At the hospital, they made me choke down liquid charcoal. I retched and retched. I remember being hooked up to an EKG and hearing a lot of erratic beeping. Eventually, I lost consciousness. I woke up in a hospital bed with an IV in my arm. I was confused and frightened. The nurse told me they had called my mother and that she was flying to see me. That made me cry. I didn't want her to come and see me like this. I didn't want my father to know, either. I wanted to just disappear and not face them or anyone.

The first meal I had that morning was Jell-O and a popsicle. It was delicious! During the week in the hospital, I got good nursing care and recovered my physical strength. But I got absolutely no counseling or psychiatric care, even though I asked if there was someone I could talk to. When my mom came, I had some comforting conversations with her. But when she left the hospital, my confusion and anxiety flared. One night, I was sure my roommate, an elderly woman, said to me, "Why don't you just jump out the window and get rid of yourself?" Or was that God talking? Fortunately, the window in our room wasn't the kind that opened. I called my mother and told her about it. She called the nurse's station and asked if I could be moved to another room. The only empty room in the hospital was an exam room, so they let me sleep there on the exam table. I didn't sleep much.

It turned out to be a very good thing that my mother came to West Virginia and stayed on campus. She brought me comfort and love. She got to meet my friends, who gathered around her and took her out for coffee and meals in the cafeteria so they could tell her how much they loved me. And she was able to advocate for me with the college administration. The college considered expelling me. She told them how much I needed to stay in school, where I could stay with the supportive friends I had made, getting the education I deserved. The college agreed, and I was allowed to stay. Why should anyone be expelled from college for having a broken brain?

On the day of my discharge from the Wheeling hospital, I had a one-minute encounter with a psychiatrist. He was a grim-faced older man and his words were harsh: "You're lucky you're not going home in a coffin on a train. Don't ever try that again." He asked no questions about why I had done it. He offered no reassurance or hope. He certainly didn't offer a referral to counseling or psychiatric care. It made me feel ashamed and hopeless.

I only told my father about the suicide attempt when I got home from college. I asked him if we could get lunch at McDonald's and eat it in the park. I was a vegetarian and got a cheeseburger without the burger. We ate it sitting on a blanket under a shady tree. It was so hard for me to tell Dad at all but it was better in person than over the phone. I knew it would make him cry. It did. He hugged me. He told me how worried he had been when he couldn't reach me for a week. (My poor roommate lied to him that I was always at the library, at a party, or out on a run). He said it hurt him to know I wanted to keep the suicide attempt a secret. He said he wanted me to always feel safe telling him hard things. I promised I would.

The miracle that I recovered from the suicide attempt and went on to graduate from Bethany College with honors certainly wasn't due to getting appropriate early intervention and care for my mental illness. That didn't happen until a decade later. I can only credit the kindness and support of my friends and peers, the love of my family, and the grace of God.

How could I live through that kind of experience and not want to pay forward the love and hope that my friends gave me? Decades later, I found a way. In 2001, my friend June Judge met me for coffee. We knew each other through the National Alliance on Mental Illness (NAMI), where I had known her to be a fierce advocate not only for her own family with mental illness, but for all of us. It felt like she was my mom, too. She told me about an organization called Compeer that seeks to lessen the loneliness and isolation of persons with mental illness by matching them with trained volunteer friends. "I saw how Compeer worked when we started a chapter in Story County, Iowa," June said. "Wouldn't it be great if we could get it going here in Johnson County? Would you help me write letters to the Robert Wood Johnson Foundation to give us a grant to launch it here?" I could never say no to June. I did write letters, many of them, and went to meetings and fought hard for this kind of equal friendship to come to life in my community.

And it worked! The grant got us through our first year, and then our hardworking board raised funds through a concert we called "The Sound of Friendship." Twenty-three years later, Compeer continues, surviving tough times like the Covid lockdown. I've been blessed by three Compeer friends: Muriel, Jackie, and now Della. We do the things persons without mental illness would take for granted: sharing meals, going on walks, shopping in thrift stores, going to Compeer socials. And we talk about anything and everything. But to persons with mental illness, this kind of connection can be hard to come by. The healing power of simple friendship is evidence-based to change lives. I've learned that wellness starts—and continues—with friendship.

The book of Ecclesiastes, said to be written by King Solomon, expresses the power of friendship:

> "Two are better than one, because they have
> a good return for their labor: If either of
> them falls down, one can help the other

up. But pity anyone who falls and has no
one to help them up."

— Ecclesiastes 4:9-10

The key of compeer true friends unlocked my loneliness and opened
the door of life.

Chapter 5

The Key of "I Wish I Were in Paris"

One of my earliest memories is a French lullaby my mother created for me. Before studying dress design, she had taken some college art classes, along with a semester of French. She made creative use of the few words she knew: "Margalea est mon amie, mon amie petite, mon amie cheri." I also give her credit for my nickname, Margalea. I was named Margaret Lea, Margaret after my paternal aunt and Lea after my maternal grandmother. I happened to live next door to Margaret Jones and Margaret Stevens, so going only by Margaret would have been very confusing. Mom blended Margaret Lea into Margalea, and I've stuck with it my whole life. The last "a" is silent, the only part of me that is.

Another language Mom introduced me to was Op-talk. I was bewildered when she and my brother would talk in it. Listening closer, I cracked the code. It was a bit like Pig Latin. You would insert "op" before every vowel. Margalea became M-op-a-gop-a-lea. It made for a lot of giggles.

When I finally did formally study a language, it was a lot harder than I thought it would be. My high school French teacher, Ms. Richardson, preferred to be known as "Madame Ree-schaar." She could be pretty strict. I remember her asking for a "voluntaire victime" (French for volunteer victim) to answer the question of what was my favorite French kind of "volaille." I thought the word meant beverage, so I timidly raised my hand and said, "le Coca Cola." She exclaimed, "Non, non, non!" I got that twice wrong—she was not asking my favorite beverage, she meant my favorite kind of poultry, and if she had meant a beverage, Coca Cola would not be the correct favorite French beverage.

The best part of high school French classes was being introduced to Antione de Saint-Exupery's fable, *The Little Prince*. It tells the story of a Little Prince who travels from planet to planet on a search for meaning and friendship. On Planet Earth, the Little Prince meets a fox who begs him to "tame" him, to become the kind of friend who was unafraid of needing the other. The fox says, "If you tame me, you will risk tears." It reminded me of how felines like Who Me had once been wild tigers but were transformed into small cats we can caress. I knew I wanted to master French well enough to travel to French-speaking countries where I might "tame" a stranger.

This was why I chose to major in journalism and French in college. Bethany College had a program with the Sorbonne in Paris. During my sophomore year, I spent August of 1978 to early January of 1979 in Paris. I worked as a part-time "au pair" in exchange for servant quarters housing in the attic of a very old building in the Latin Quarter. Things got off on the wrong foot when I struggled to pronounce the children's names: Eight-year-old Marie Adelaide, six-year-old Marie Elodie, and two-year-old Gautier mocked me until I finally caught on. To make matters worse, I didn't understand their idioms. When Gautier said, "I must make an apple," I quickly learned that it meant he had to go potty. When Marie Elodie said, "My heart hurts," I tried to reassure her she was too young for heart trouble. But then she spit up on me. Aha! As I cleaned her up, I added the idiom to my vocabulary.

And even at that young age, they were class-conscious. You could say they were "born with a silver spoon in their mouths." One of my duties was to mix grenadine syrup and water in each of the children's silver christening cups. And when Gautier happened to drop the spoon, he told me, "You're the servant girl; you pick it up."

This wasn't the kind of cross-cultural friendship I was hoping for. But Paris was so much bigger than three spoiled children, and I was only a part-time servant, working on weekday afternoons, free on weekends, with breaks for Christmas and New Year from the Sorbonne. I explored the city, taking "le Metro" everywhere, and enjoyed museums and cathedrals. At the Sorbonne, I met international students and tasted foods they shared that were new to me, like couscous, tofu, and curry. My friend Martha, an au pair with cleaning duties in Germany, visited me in Paris. I asked Madame if Martha could use the family shower, and she responded, "Why? She's only going to be here for a week."

On my Christmas break, I took an all-night train to the Taizé monastery in the south of France. I remember walking into the monastery welcome building and being served a most comforting cup of hot chocolate. They fed me simple, delicious meals and let me sleep in bunk beds in cabins without charge, which was a blessing because I had spent most of my money on the train fare. I rehearsed with the choir singing chants in Greek, Latin, French, Spanish, and German before the Christmas Eve Midnight Mass. At 11:59, we sang, "Maranatha, Maranatha" (Come, Lord, Come). Then the bells rang out, and we sang, "Alleluia! Alleluia!" I hugged the other choir members, even though I had only known them for a few days. Christmas had come, and we couldn't be strangers anymore.

To this day, I still love those Taizé hymns and am blessed by a local church that has a Taizé service monthly. The kindness of strangers in France and later in Canada, when I studied at Laval University in Quebec City, made human connections that crossed barriers of language and culture. When you sing in a community in diverse languages, minds and hearts unite.

When I am lonely and sad, I close my eyes and return to my mother's lullaby. I remember that I am a friend, and a dear one, to many people. I try to speak to myself with the same respectful language I would use with a friend. That's why I named one of my keys to wellness, "I wish I were in Paris." I try to redirect myself from saying out of frustration, "I wish I were dead." Because I don't really wish I were dead. I wish I could make a fresh start on a wild new adventure as if I were in Paris trying new foods—something beyond "le Coca Cola." While I'm there, I'll be "taming" new friends. I'll take the risk of weeping in the hope of finding a true friend.

Chapter 6

An Off-Key Mind

My brain at age 21, just out of college, had not reached maturity. It is well established that the brain undergoes a rewiring process that is not complete until approximately 25 years of age. I give myself grace for that.

After graduating from Bethany College in West Virginia, I returned to the Washington, D.C., area. I wasn't clear on what would come next. I had earned degrees in French and journalism, but how was I going to use what I had learned? Going through the classified ads in the *Washington Post* didn't turn up a job opening for *"foreign journalist wanted, no experience necessary, haute couture wardrobe provided."* I felt like an imposter for graduating with honors but not being a professional journalist upon graduation.

If I could talk to my younger self, I would tell her: *"God gave you the gift of writing and storytelling. God will open doors for you if you stay persistent and don't give up. The WHY behind your college education was not to know everything; it was to learn how to learn. Just think of all the beautiful mystery you have yet to learn."*

I had earned money for college over four summers working for a secretarial temp agency. I knew I was a fast, accurate typist (this was before PCs) and that I was good at answering phone calls. My mom asked me to help pay the rent for the apartment we shared, and I wanted to be a responsible wage earner. Sewing together with my mom, I had some clothing that made me feel professional. Mom had gone from dress design school to becoming a draftsman and a graphic artist. If she could learn on the job, so could I. Maybe after earning some money, I could travel and write more creatively.

I went to an employment agency and asked for help finding work as a secretary. They sent me on an interview with a small non-profit agency called the National Jogging Association (NJA). General Richard L. Bohanon founded the NJA (Later American Running and Fitness Association) in 1968, and by the early 1980s, jogging had really caught on. The group sought to encourage beginning joggers to become runners and seasoned runners to run marathons. The NJA had a monthly newsletter. They were looking for a membership coordinator to send bulk mailings and handle subscriptions. They encouraged their employees to run during their lunch hours and provided a dressing room and shower to freshen up afterward. The office was in the Foggy Bottom neighborhood of Washington, D.C., near the Potomac River. The salary wasn't high, but there were health benefits, using a new model called an HMO (Health Management Organization). It didn't occur to me that having an HMO meant I couldn't keep seeing my family doctor but would have to be treated by providers who were strangers to me. The job seemed like a good fit for me. When I got their call offering the position, I accepted it immediately.

On my first day on the job, I was oriented to using a computer the size of a washing machine to manage the membership database. There were a lot of glitches. My dad used to joke, "To err is human; to really screw things up takes a computer." Once, when we were sending out letters to US state governors asking them to proclaim Running and

Fitness Day in their states, the merge fields got shifted. The governor of Virginia was asked to declare the day in the state of Washington, and so on. We caught it in time, but what a mess!

It helped me deal with the stress of computer chaos to jog on my lunch hour. I would eat a light lunch before changing clothes and running past the Watergate Hotel and along the Potomac River. I had never been very athletic in high school or college. I hated PE class, especially sports like volleyball, where I was afraid of the ball hitting my eyeglasses. My favorite exercise was walking leisurely, my mind caught up with writing projects or books I was reading. But now that running was part of my job, I became more disciplined. I ran in a couple of 5K races. I remember being cheered on by a bystander while running the Bonnie Bell 5K. He shouted, "You're strong, can't go wrong." I liked the sound of that.

I'm so glad this job helped me make exercise a healthy habit in my early twenties. By my thirties, I gained a lot of weight, especially with the side effects of some of the medicines I was on. But joining Weight Watchers in 1997 helped me recommit to fitness. Now, in my mid-sixties, I wear a fitness tracker and aim for 10,000 steps or more daily. I don't run anymore because it's too hard on my knees, but I walk briskly, exercise using "walk at home" videos, lift weights, and practice tai chi. I thank God for my body and how it has carried me through life. I want to have a fit body all the days I'm blessed to live.

A year passed on the new job. My friend Martha and I ran in the Diabetes Derby, wearing funny plastic hats. I posed in photographs doing stretching exercises for the jogger group's newsletter. I enjoyed using my talent for calligraphy in crafting certificates that we sent to members for reaching mileage goals. I got along with my boss and coworkers. I was especially close to the mailroom clerk, Tom, who was also a college graduate. He told me he was comfortable with a less stressful job, even if the pay wasn't great. I shared my writing with him, and he affirmed it. Everything was great.

Except it wasn't.

Even with the endorphins I was generating from all the aerobic exercise, I was still sad and anxious. I couldn't run away from this pervasive, numb hopelessness. I was sleeping poorly, sometimes falling asleep on my ride and missing my Metro stop, which made me late for work.

In my last year of college, I lost two fellow students to suicide. I wasn't terribly close to either one of them, but the way they ended their lives was triggering to me. It was like leaving the door open in the middle of a violent windstorm and not being able to push it shut. If people my age could hurt so much that they ended their lives, was there any hope for me to get through the challenges of being a young adult and go on living?

One day in August of 1982, right before I went on a lunch hour run, I left a note on Tom's desk. I wrote, "Thank you for being a friend. I hope you will remember me as a good person. I need to escape my life now. This is goodbye." I left the office and jogged more slowly than usual, my feet heavy as lead.

I felt like it wasn't me in my own body doing the running. I could hear a voice that wasn't my own voice echoing in my mind. More voices joined in, some male and some female, some low and some loud. They were growling, threatening me like a wild animal. They told me I had to do what they said, or they would torture me.

Something about these voices was familiar. Where had I heard them before? I traveled back in memory to when I was a small child, sick in bed one summer afternoon. The house was quiet, except for the soothing whirring of my mother's sewing machine. My bedroom curtains were billowing with a breeze. Or were there monsters with tentacles clawing through the windows? I heard hissing, growling, shouting. I called out.

Mommy came rushing into my room. "What's wrong, sweetie?" she asked. I said, "There are monsters. They are mean. They want me dead. Can't you hear them?"

"No, I can't hear anything. It's all right, honey, I'm here. You must have a fever." She gave me a baby aspirin and cooled me off with a cotton ball dipped in a bottle of perfume she had chilled in the refrigerator. Some mothers might have used rubbing alcohol, but the perfume was nicer.

But my mom was far away now. I was far from any help. The voices commanded me to drown in the river. I couldn't say no to them. Or could I? If I couldn't say no to them, couldn't I have at least said, "Not now." Later, I learned to say, "I'm too busy dancing life to die right now." But I didn't have the courage to say that yet. So, I did what the bullying voices said to do.

The river was muddy and had a stench to it. I was repelled by it. Our bodies have a built-in aversion to danger and death. I hesitated. I tried to pull back. I took a big step in, then another step. I waded in up to my waist. Then I went in deeper. But instead of drowning as the voices commanded me to, I began to sweep with my arms and kick with my legs, doing a strong breaststroke. My body remembered all those swimming lessons my mother made sure I had. I recently came across a card saying that I qualified as an Advanced Beginner in Swimming, dated August 26, 1966, when I would have been six years old. What a mysterious grace that my body remembered how to stay alive and did so whether my distorted thinking wanted me to or not!

I reached one of the first arches of the nearby bridge, turned around, and swam to shore. Then, I climbed out and back up to the sidewalk and started walking back to the office.

Tom came running down the sidewalk toward me, shouting my name. I must have been a horrifying sight, my clothing plastered to my body, my hair covered in mud, my mouth wide open in shock. "What happened to you?" Tom asked. "Were you trying to kill yourself? I'm so glad you stayed. Come on, let's go back to the office and get you cleaned up." We walked back together, his arm in a sideways hug around my shoulder.

After I showered and changed, I was called into my boss Maggie's office for a one-on-one meeting. Maggie was a tall, lean woman who ran marathons. She was a good boss, a mentor encouraging my work and my running. She had just given me a raise a month earlier. She told me she was very concerned about what Tom told her had just happened. She asked me if I had meant to commit suicide.

I denied it, lying, saying, "I was hot, and I wanted to go for a swim."

She said, "That's nonsense. You need to talk to someone about your reckless actions. I'm making you an appointment with a psychiatrist in our HMO plan."

"There's nothing wrong with me. This is none of your business," I shouted back. "You can't make me do that."

"If you don't do it, I can fire you for insubordination."

I knew she meant what she said. I was frightened by the consequences of not following through with the appointment.

The next day, I took a taxi to the HMO clinic. I sat across from the doctor, my eyes looking first down at my lap and then up toward the ceiling. I didn't volunteer any information and answered her questions with monosyllables. All she knew about me was what my employer told her when she made the appointment. I was bewildered when she said, "I'd like to put you on a medicine called an antidepressant." What? There are pills for your emotions? I wasn't going to have anything to do with it. I stood up and walked out the door.

If my brain had been a piano, it would have desperately needed a tuning. But, if you don't have an ear to perceive your thinking is off-key, you go on making music so lacking in harmony that it makes hearing people cover their ears.

The people who loved me, including my boss and coworkers, had to point me to helpers because I had no ear for my off-key thinking. I needed to receive that help before I could understand how desperately I needed it. There is a medical term called "anosognosia," which means a patient with schizophrenia can be blocked in their understanding of their own condition. Even people who don't have schizophrenia find it hard to get insight.

Though this was one of the most dissonant times in my young adult life, a higher power concert director was raising a baton--one quiet pause before directing a symphony. Perhaps it would be Schubert's unfinished symphony. I would have to wait years to hear it.

Chapter 7

On Being Locked Out of My Mind

I am writing this chapter on Labor Day, 2023, 41 years after I got locked out of my mind.

I told my boss, "I quit," after that infuriating visit with the HMO psychiatrist. I returned to the headhunters, asking for a job with a more professional challenge. My boss at NJA must have given me a good reference despite my leaving on short notice because the agency placed me almost immediately as a secretary at a national nonprofit. My desk was in an open area surrounded by other desks. The phone lines lit up like fireworks, and I couldn't keep up. Callers yelled at me for cutting them off. When I fled to the restroom for privacy, I had to take a key on a key chain the size of a ping-pong paddle and walk through the maze of desks and offices down a long hallway. I was sure I was being watched and spied on.

Unlike the old job, there was no dressing room or shower to make it practical to go for a run, but I was so desperate to get exercise that I ran in my dress, nylons, and high heels. I got sweaty and smelly. The aerobic exercise brought me no endorphins. The office was in the business district, far from the Potomac River, which I missed even though I had almost died there. Each day the voices got louder, growling obscenities and telling me I was a failure and a fool. I thought it was my boss and coworkers saying those things because it was so real to my ears. This job *challenge* was feeling more like job *torture*. I found myself wishing to have my old job back. But that bridge was burned.

I was only on the new job five days before Labor Day weekend. Martha and I had planned to spend the three-day weekend visiting our friend Mary at the Norfolk, Virginia, Navy Base. Mary was married with three children, and her husband, Don, was at sea. I took the subway and bus home to Hyattsville, Maryland, where I shared an apartment with Martha and two other girlfriends. Martha was eager to get on the road for the over 200-mile trip as soon as possible. We ran into a lot of traffic, and it was late when we got to Mary's house. Her young children, DJ, Brian, and Tammy, were already in bed.

I remember Mary showing us the children's toys, including Care Bears, which had just come out on the market. They had names that were supposed to help children express their emotions, like Cheer Bear and Grumpy Bear. If I had been a Care Bear, my name would have been Un-Sleepy Bear or Dark Thinking Bear. After we said goodnight to Mary, Martha and I laid down on sleeping bags in the living room. I tossed and turned and muttered to myself. Wolves chased me, but I was unable to scream. I may have awakened screaming. With my eyes wide open, I saw my dead body being pulled from the river, gray and bloated. I heard prayers at my funeral and then voices shouting, "She deserved to die."

On Saturday afternoon, Martha drove me to nearby Virginia Beach to connect with a man with whom I had exchanged letters. This was 1982, long before online dating. We met through a group called Single Book Lovers Club, where participants named their five favorite books as indications of what kind of date you might be. I think one of the books this man and I had in common was the Bible. His last letter said, "Meet me at the Norwegian statue on the board-walk." Martha drove around and around, unable to find parking, and let me out of the car to search for the statue. I ran up and down the boardwalk shouting, "Mr. Single Booklover, it's me, Margalea." (Actually, I called him by his real name, but that name is forever unclaimed in Memory Lost and Found). He must have recognized me from the snapshot I had mailed him because he called out, "Over here, Margalea." He invited me to climb on the back of his motorcy-cle. He gave me a helmet to put on. I wrapped my arms around him, and we thundered away to a steakhouse restaurant, which was a lovely idea, except that I was a vegetarian. I picked at a salad. He did most of the talking as I was distracted by the voices calling me names. Then we got back on his motorcycle and went to Mary's house. Mary and Martha gave us privacy in the living room. I remember the living room being darkened.

What did we do in that dim lighting? Did we hold hands? Did we kiss and neck? I don't remember any sense of pleasure or attraction. I don't remember any guilt for making out with someone I had barely met. I don't remember his name, his hair color, or if he wore tight jeans or manly aftershave. I only remember a bewildered numbness. I do have some puzzle pieces that I can put together to tell me some-thing: He was kind. He was kind to arrange our first meeting in a public place. He was kind to give me a motorcycle helmet to wear when I rode with him. He was kind not to take me back to his apart-ment or to take advantage of me that way. We both had the Bible in common on our Single Book Lover profiles and maybe that is what made him respect me, his tormented neighbor, as himself. We said goodnight, and we were never in contact again.

The memories of that weekend are perplexing. I asked Martha what she remembered. She distinctly recalled my three nights of sleepless agitation. She said that on Sunday morning, we attended services at Granby Avenue Church of Christ near the naval base in Norfolk.

Mary and her three young children came with us. At this point, if I could pray at all, it was with groans too deep for words. So, thank you, Martha and Mary, all these years later, for your prayers.

On the way back from Mary's, Martha took me to Kensington, Maryland, to my mom's apartment, having called ahead to let my mother know I was not myself. Mom opened the door, her face creased with worry. She and Martha talked with each other in low voices. I was so numb, I didn't care if they were talking about me. I have a gap in memory about what followed. Mom said I was babbling nonsense like, "River vomit kiss me why?" The psychiatric term for this kind of speech is "word salad." Well, I was a vegetarian and a writer, so why wouldn't I make a salad out of words? My mother didn't see any humor in it at the time. I told her I was a failure at the new job and could never work again. I said that I wasn't going to kill myself, but I *was* going to be executed by God.

I finally did sleep for an hour or so. Tuesday morning, Mom knocked on my bedroom door and told me to get dressed. I insisted on phoning the new boss to say I resigned, even though Mom tried to keep me from doing so. She wanted to tell them herself that I was not well and needed disability leave. She didn't want me to be without health insurance. I dialed the phone anyway and kept it together long enough to ask to be transferred to my boss. When she got on the line, I spit out, "We no more, you bitch." I hung up the phone and sobbed. Mom tried to calm me down, saying we needed to go to our family doctor. I had no energy left to fight her about it.

Mom opened the car door, and I got in, but I wouldn't fasten my seat belt. She reached over and fastened it for me. I had always enjoyed riding in the green Dodge Colt that we named "Little Leaf," but there was no joy in it this time. Mom rolled down the windows to let in some air because it was a hot day. She started driving down University Boulevard. The dashes on the highway were hissing at me like snakes.

Since my parents split, Dr. S. had cared for me and my mom. Mom researched female doctors who take a holistic approach. Even in my mental chaos, I sensed I could trust her. Her graying hair felt grand-motherly. But I still didn't say much in response to her questions.

Dr. S. said, "Margalea, you don't seem like yourself. Could you be on drugs or alcohol?"

I said a forceful, "No."

She asked me to step out of the room while she talked to Mom privately. In the waiting room, I was trembling with fear. What were they going to do with me? Was wanting to take your life a crime punishable by death?

Dr. S. opened the exam room door and ushered me inside.

"Margalea," she said, "I am going to admit you to the hospital."

What did she mean by *admit*? Is *admit* confessing a falsehood? How could you *admit* someone else's shame? I didn't have much time to ask her to explain before Mom and I got back in the car and went to Suburban Hospital in Bethesda.

My mother dragged me out of the car and into the hospital lobby. I was shouting, "I hate you for bringing me here." But when we took the elevator up to the fourth floor and came up to the nurse's station, I changed my tune.

"Don't leave me here." I wailed.

The nurse said to my mother, "She can't have visitors until she's stabi-lized. It could be a few days."

Mom handed the nurse my suitcase. She gave me a sideways hug. "You're going to be all right," she said. "I love you."

"If you really loved me, you wouldn't leave me here," I growled.

She turned and left.

I feel so sad for my mother that day. She did the right thing getting me professional help. My illness had to bring to mind the dementia that my mother's mother struggled with toward the end of her life. Once, my maternal grandmother was restrained to her bed by hospital nurses; that had to be so cruel for my mom to witness. Mom told me how once her mother talked to her as if she were a stranger, speaking in the third person, saying, "Eleanor (my mom) was the hardest child I ever raised."

My mom herself was no stranger to depression. She wrote an essay for the Church of the Saviour newsletter in the 1960s about imagining herself on a raft in the middle of the ocean, unsure if she wanted to stay on the raft and live or let go of the raft and drown. She was a courageous woman, a seeker of truth. I am proud to be her daughter. I am also proud to be my grandmother's granddaughter. The three of us are a chain of life. Even though I have never given birth myself, I carry life forward.

I wish my arms today were long enough to reach back four decades to hold her in a long, tight hug. I would promise her that I would commit to getting well, finding my hidden key, and unlocking my mind.

Chapter 8

The Key of Finding a Job to Do

I didn't unlock anything that first day in the hospital. It didn't help that the first thing I was told to do was change into a hospital gown and bathrobe, which made me shiver. And then, having a physical exam performed by a young male doctor made me feel even more locked out of my own private body.

Later, I had a baffling interview with a psychiatrist, who introduced himself as Dr. W. He was a gray-haired man with kind eyes. For some reason, I trusted him, even though he was a stranger and asked odd questions. The questions about my name and age made sense, but why did he need me to remember the words "orange, tobacco, and ball?" (I only remember them now because they are a psychiatric intake interview cliché that I've since heard repeatedly). Why did he want me to count backward from a hundred by threes? I refused to even try to do so, saying I wasn't any good at math. But the weirdest question he asked was, "What is the meaning of the saying, 'People in glass houses shouldn't throw stones?'"

I said, "Are you asking that question because I am in a glass house? Is that why I feel like my enemies are watching my every move? I knew they were watching me when they made me change out of my own clothing and put on the hospital gown. They saw that my bare skin was thin and that my naked body was ugly. If you give me a stone, I'll throw it at them. But that would break the window from the inside, and more cold air would come in, making me colder and more scared. I need you to help me build a better house. I can't tell you anything more because the voices say they will kill me if I tell their secrets."

There was a little more discussion, which was even fuzzier in my mind, and then he walked me back to the psych floor. I returned to my room, a single room with one bed and a rocking chair. I rocked back and forth, giggling, "I'm not off my rocker!"

I couldn't figure out why our food was served on Styrofoam plates with plastic silverware at lunch. After lunch, I sat in the day room watching television for a while. There was a new television hospital drama called *Saint Elsewhere*. I knew of a Washington, D.C. psychiatric hospital called Saint Elizabeth's Hospital. Was this show trying to tell me I would be sent to Saint Elizabeth if I didn't get better in a hurry? Then dinner was served on more Styrofoam plates. After dinner, I decided to stay away from the scary television. I sat at a table in the dining room where some nurses were on their break. One of them was showing off snapshots of her grandchildren to the others. It made me feel that they were kind nurses to be around. Then they returned to work, and I wasn't sure what to do next. I decided to go back to my room, but I couldn't sleep.

At about eight o'clock, the loudspeaker said that patients needed to get in line at the nurse's station. A nurse came into my room to make sure I did so. Why did I need to do this? I got in the back of the line, four or five patients ahead of me. When I got to the window, I was handed a little paper cup with pills in it and a cup of water.

I said, "I think there's a mistake; I don't take any medicine."

"You need to take it; your doctor prescribed it," the nurse said.

"But why?"

"If you don't take the pills, we'll give you an injection. Take the pills."

I tipped the cup into my mouth and washed the pills down with water. The nurse made me open my mouth and stick out my tongue to prove I had indeed swallowed them.

I returned to my room and lay on the bed, feeling defeated and stuck.

Days passed, each one much like the one before. More meals on Styrofoam plates. More visits with the psychiatrist. More pills in little paper cups. More spooky television, which I learned to avoid. Saliva started pooling in my mouth, and if I didn't pay attention, I drooled. Jerky movements of my face and arms began plaguing me. They gave me more pills for that, saying it was a side effect of the first pills.

The voices went from pounding on my skull to being more like a loud party in the next room. Psychotherapy was still confusing. It felt good to be listened to, even though I was still lost.

I was considered stable enough to have visitors. My parents came to see me separately. They were amicably divorced and committed to working together to care for me, but it was still better for them to come alone and be one-on-one with me.

Mom came. Years later, she told me she was shocked by how flat and numb I seemed, and she wondered if I was really on the proper medication. I don't remember much about our visits, but I remember her telling me every time before she left, "Be the stubborn Altenberg you were born to be." "Altenberg" was the name of the German ancestors on my mother's side of the family, and she believed a little German stubbornness could help me fight for my life.

Dad came and read me the Sunday comics from the *Washington Post*. I couldn't read them myself because blurred vision was a medication side effect. I didn't get the punch lines, but I smiled a half smile because my father's voice reading them was so amusing.

Both my parents and my half-brother David came to family psychotherapy meetings. Because Dr. W.'s approach was to look for hidden trauma and abuse, these sessions were agonizing and did more harm than good. They usually ended with me screaming hysterically and my parents fighting tears.

The truth was that my family loved me as best they knew how. Mom loved me by taking care of my finances. She got the National Jogging Association to continue my health insurance to help cover the bill for my long hospitalization. And almost miraculously, she also got me on Social Security Disability Income. My father loved me with humor and prayer. David took me on passes to walk through the park. He shared with me an encouraging Alcoholics Anonymous affirmation, "I thank God for my health."

How I wish my family had found the grassroots advocacy group, National Alliance on Mental Illness (NAMI), at the onset of my mental health battle. NAMI started as a small group of families gathered around a kitchen table in 1979 and blossomed into the nation's leading voice on mental health. My family could have taken a NAMI Family to Family class. In this ten-week class, they would have found information and strategies for caring for me. They would also have found out they were not alone. They would learn that recovery is a journey, and that there is help. But they didn't get that kind of help.

As the weeks passed, my fingers were always tap, tap, tapping on an invisible typewriter. I told Dr. W. I needed to go back to work. He wrote a note on a prescription pad that said, "Give Margalea a job to do," and told me to give it to a nurse. The nurse I gave it to rolled her eyes. She reached into the linen cart, pulled out a washcloth, and handed it to me. She said, "Okay, Margalea, you can wash the wall." I washed the wall diligently for hours.

Emotionally, I did the work of mental health recovery diligently as well. As my journey went forward, I came to recognize how important the keys of medication and psychotherapy were. My recovery might have gone more smoothly if I'd found education, advocacy, and support from NAMI. As it was, no one educated me about my diagnosis and why I was taking the medications I was forced to take. I wish the kind of psychotherapy I was getting had not been focused on the past and on blaming my family. It would have been more productive to keep it in the here and now and focus on the preventive factors of a happy childhood and a loving family.

After a month and a half at Suburban Hospital, I was discharged to Day Treatment at Washington Adventist Hospital. One of the nurses opened the locked door of the psychiatric floor and let me out, accompanied by my mother. I was proud that this was one locked door I had worked hard to put behind me.

Chapter 9

The Key of Ancient Airs and Dances

"The tragedy is not that things are broken. The tragedy is that things are not mended again."

— Alan Paton, *Cry, The Beloved Country*

I was able to transition from inpatient at Suburban to day treatment at Washington Adventist Hospital because Martha's parents, Ken and Helen Foster, opened their home and their hearts to me. I was too fragile to live alone, and both my parents worked full-time and couldn't give me the supervision I needed. The Fosters said they would happily have me live with them for a few months. It was poetic that their last name was Foster, and they were offering me a kind of foster care.

I had stayed at the Fosters' home several times before. During junior high and high school, Martha and I would hang out together on week-ends or snow days. Martha always offered to sleep in the top bunk, in case that was awkward for me, not being used to a bunk bed, but I insisted I was fine. One night, I dreamed that I had to run across the street to escape an oncoming car. I moved my legs and fell right out of bed. I must not have tensed up as I fell because I landed softly on my left side, bewildered by what had just happened.

Martha jumped out of bed, asking, "Margalea, are you all right?"

I just giggled. "I'm fine. How the heck did I do that?"

Years later, when Martha was married and the mother of a daughter, Rachel, and a son, David, her children would ask her to, "Tell us again the story about the time Aunt Margalea fell out of bed."

The Fosters had also hosted me for a week when my mother was in the hospital with digestive problems when I was about fifteen years old.

Then and now, their kind hospitality to me was a blessing. Especially having just recently been an inpatient, I appreciated the structure and routine of my days there. Mrs. Foster would tap on my door in the morning to wake me up for breakfast so I would be ready when my father came to drive me to Day Treatment at Washington Adventist Hospital every weekday morning.

By now, it was mid-fall with short days and colder temperatures. When I got in Dad's car, he had the heater on, and that felt cozy. The ride to the hospital took us past a park with a creek. Watching the water splash over the rocks distracted me in a good way. I still heard voices, but they weren't as loud in tormenting me. Dad would tune in to WETA on the car radio. WETA was a public radio channel that played classical music, which was the style of music both my parents enjoyed the most and that I had grown up with. The theme song of the program that began at nine o'clock was the first few measures of Respighi's "Ancient Airs and Dances." Morning after morning, we listened together in silence. I didn't pay close attention to the music, but it was soothing and soon became part of my new normal routine.

The day treatment program was another new normal. There was music time, games, support groups, and meals. Because the hospital was sponsored by the Adventist church, all the meals were vegetarian, except they were processed to look and taste like meat. It was an odd experience to eat "meatloaf with gravy" that contained no meat.

Dad brought me back to the Fosters' about four in the afternoon.

Mrs. Foster had me help her with some of the preparations of supper. She reminded me to wash my hands. She had me use a brush to scrub mushrooms, saying "mushrooms grow in dung." My appetite improved because I helped prepare the food I was eating.

Mr. Foster came home from work about 5:30 and we'd sit down to eat. After supper and putting dirty dishes in the dishwasher, we went to the living room and sat quietly and read. Mrs. Foster was a children's librarian, and she had a lot of children's books on the shelves, including the Laura Ingalls Wilder *Little House* series. My vision was blurry from medication side effects and the large print was easier for me to read. This was so much better for me than watching television with all its confusing images and sounds.

Despite my progress, the undercurrent of my illness sucked me back under and spiraled me back to giving up hope. The Fosters trusted me to take my psychiatric medication and the bottle was kept in their medicine cabinet in the bathroom. The bottle was half empty. I tipped the contents of the bottle into my hand and popped the pills into my mouth. This was a weekday morning; I went about my routine as if nothing had happened, eating breakfast with the Fosters and riding with Dad to Day Treatment. We probably listened to WETA's upbeat music, but I found no pleasure in doing so.

At Day Treatment, I kept waiting for the pills to have some effect on me, but I didn't notice anything. In the support group, I finally confessed what I had done. Apparently, the kind of medicine I'd taken was not very toxic, and the amount I took was small enough that the staff wasn't concerned about taking me to the ER or giving me any emetics. They called it a suicidal "gesture," but *were* concerned enough that they admitted me to the Washington Adventist Psych floor.

I spent Christmas as an inpatient there. A church choir came and sang carols. The one that made me feel the most despondent was the song, "I'll be home for Christmas... if only in my dreams."

Martha's mother gave me a Christmas present of the 1948 novel by Alan Paton, *Cry, The Beloved Country*. At first, I couldn't imagine why she would give me such a tragic story. It was a narrative about a Zulu pastor and his son, Absolom, set against the background of a land and a people riven by racial injustice. It ends with the father watching from a distance as Absolom is executed for the murder of a white man. Not exactly "happily ever after." But as I kept reading about sadness that was greater than my own, it lifted my spirits a little. While it's rarely helpful to compare someone else's suffering as greater or lesser than our own, hearing stories of others who endure suffering and still persevere is a way of growing along with them.

Another benefit of *Cry, The Beloved Country* was that it gave me empathy for my family, especially my father. How hard it would be for him if I took my life!

The inpatient stay was short, and I returned to the Fosters and my daily routine there, including the WETA theme song that had become a theme song for my closeness with my father. One morning, I surprised my father—and myself—by humming along. The music buzzed through me. My very bones vibrated. My head nodded with the beat. My toes did a little tapping. This wasn't the jerky movement side effects of my medication. This wasn't typing on an invisible typewriter. This movement was a dance bursting through the locked doors of my despair and relapses.

I would soon be discharged from the Day Treatment program. It was like moving on to the next dance.

Chapter 10

The Key of the House of the Lord

As a young child, I considered the building where my family worshipped my family castle. The church purchased the brownstone Victorian-style building at 2025 Massachusetts Avenue, NW Washington, D.C., in 1950, nine years before I was born. Hours of volunteer labor had transformed a run-down family mansion, built in 1885, into a house of worship. Rising to the right of the building was a three-story tower with a pointed roof. Inside were 25 rooms with tall ceilings. The formal rooms had carpeted stairs with gallery balconies looking down on the main hall. The "servant stairs" were winding wooden steps that went from the basement to the attic. This was where I first learned to climb stairs because our family home was all one level. The sweet smell of Murphy's Oil soap always brings back memories of polished wood paneling gleaming in chandelier light. Light shone through stained glass windows that weren't religious pictures but Art Deco floral patterns with deep pink and purple petals.

When I got old enough to read, I learned the brass sign to the left of the front door said, *Headquarters of Church of the Saviour.* The church founders deliberately used the word "headquarters" to make it clear that the church was the living body of believers, not the building. I was much older before I understood the unique qualities of this church, founded in 1947 to be an ecumenical church praying and working for the healing of divisions among Christians. My parents were attracted to it in the late 1950s, having read about it in a Christian magazine (*Guideposts?*). Pastor Gordon Cosby baptized me as a one-year-old, and Bill and Lolly Shiflett became my Godparents. Later in life, I would be baptized again as a young adult. Being an ecumenical church meant that the Church of the Saviour didn't have any hard and fast doctrine about baptism.

Some of my earliest memories are being in a preschool Sunday School class in the damp-smelling basement with teacher Lou Longfellow playing music on a record player for us to dance the Hokey Pokey. It may not have taught us about the Bible, but it did teach us to enjoy the gift of our bodies. Another Sunday School teacher must have been at the end of her rope, so she took our class to a nearby park and told us she would give us a dollar for every pigeon we caught. We ran around in circles chasing the poor birds, and she never had to shell out a dollar. After Sunday School, the children had refreshments in the kitchen. We were allowed to pour ourselves plastic cups of Rock Creek brand soda; my favorite was cream soda. But things got out of hand when one of the boys shook a bottle of soda and sprayed the kitchen walls with it. Others joined in. I shouldn't have, but I probably did anyway. We were sternly scolded and it didn't happen again. I think we had to wash the walls with paper towels.

Children had Sunday School classes while adults and older children worshipped separately. I worshipped in the chapel for the first time in my early teens. The chapel was a long, narrow room that had been added onto the building by the church. It was the most simple and unadorned room in the whole building. The chapel doors opened in the middle of the room, facing the altar. Above the altar was a rough-hewn wooden cross. To the left and right of the altar were ten rows of chairs on each side. There were six chairs in each row, separated by a middle aisle so that people could walk to their seats. A church member had crafted the wooden chairs with woven wicker seats which, frankly, were rather uncomfortable, making the service seem longer to me as a young person. I did like the poetic imagery and cadence of the liturgy. Gordon Cosby's preaching was powerful; he varied his voice from shouting to whispering. He'd clear his throat frequently and that gave you a moment to absorb what he'd just said. The hymnal was a Mennonite one, something that eased my transition into becoming a Mennonite later in life.

About the time my parents split, Church of the Saviour broke into sister communities, and my mother and I attended Seekers Church of the Saviour and my father attended Ecumenical Church of the Saviour. Seekers had a teenaged Sunday School class and I found belonging there with my peers.

During my senior year of high school, I got permission to spend a personal retreat day in the building so that I could ponder my life path, including whether to go to college and what to study. It was a Saturday and I pretty much had the place to myself. I brought bath towels and soap so that I could do something I had always wanted to do—take a bath in the claw-foot bathtub on the second floor. It had probably not been used for over 60 years. That afternoon, I painted a mural on the attic wall with calligraphy letters spelling out a verse from *The Desiderata* poem by Max Ehmann: "Beyond a wholesome discipline, be gentle with yourself. You are a child of the universe no less than the trees and the stars; you have a right to be here."

After my day of retreat, I found the discernment I needed to decide to attend Bethany College. On summer breaks and after college, I continued to worship at Church of the Saviour and take classes in

The School of Christian Living. The church's mission became more tangible to me. The church continues to flourish to this day. Their web page says, "The Church of the Saviour lives out its call to the inward/outward journey together in different communities. Each has a distinct charisma and style, but all share the tradition of deep commitment, listening for God's leading, and servant ministry in the nation's capital."

The onset of mental illness fractured my belief in God and made faith a harder concept to grasp. I remember Pastor Sonya Dyer visiting me once at Suburban Hospital. I think I may have yelled obscenities at her. But my church community didn't give up on me. They kept lifting me up in prayer and being a support to my parents. At one point, Seeker's Community of Church of the Saviour helped pay one of my hospital bills.

As I emerged from my two hospitalizations, my mind began to reopen itself to belief. The castle of my childhood church home became a nest of support. Psalm 84:3 describes God's house as a place where *"even the sparrow has found a home, and the swallow a nest for herself, where she may have her young—a place near your altar, Lord Almighty, my King and my God."*

I was like a mother bird caring for my many selves, selves that were fighting for belonging and purpose. The first widening of my circle of support was finding a place to live somewhat independently but surrounded by community. Alfred Rose, who owned a three-story house on Porter Street in Northwest Washington, invited men and women from Church of the Saviour to live with him in intentional Christian community. Three men and two women were the first members of the household. I had explored living there before my mental health crisis, and they held a place for me while I was at my most ill. They were willing to accept that I didn't have much income to pay rent. At this point, I had lost my disability income and was living on what my parents could afford to share with me.

The next miracle was finding a job that used my gifts and accommodated my needs as a mentally disabled person. This was seven years before the passage of the Americans with Disabilities Act (ADA). Persons like me who had mental disabilities (although I prefer to call myself differently abled) had no civil right to employment that accommodated their needs. I had a big gap in my resume that was hard to explain. I recognized I could not go back to the same employment agency that had placed me in the last nightmare secretarial job. Fortunately, Church of the Saviour had recently opened an employment agency called Jubilee Jobs. Their mission then and continuing to this day is "to provide professional, compassionate job placement into marketplace jobs for persons eager and ready to work."

I took the D.C. Metrobus to their office. I wore one of the suits that my mother had made me that I felt professional wearing. I hope that I had showered, though my grooming skills had slipped over the past months. I checked in with a friendly receptionist, who gave me a typing test, which I aced with 70 words a minute with very few errors. There was a test of proofreading skills, which I also did well on.

I was soon ushered into the office of Terry Flood, a church member I had known for years and whose children I had babysat. Instead of a handshake, she asked if she could give me a hug. I said, "Yes!"

"Margalea, I'm so glad you've come to us. I know you've been having a hard time and that you've been discharged from a psychiatric hospitalization recently. Tell me more about how you are feeling now."

"I've been discharged from inpatient and day treatment care. I've got a nice place to live. I really want to work, and I need an income. I'm a great typist, and I'd love to get my hands on an electric typewriter."

"It sounds like you're motivated to work and that you've got some real strengths to share. What things are hard for you?"

"I'm doing a lot better, but some things are still hard for me. I can't go back to a job where I must answer a whole lot of phone lines. I have trouble getting up in the morning because of my psych meds, and I'd like to have a job with flexible hours. If I could have a somewhat private office to work in, I would feel safer and more confident."

"I think I might have a job that would fit with your strengths and needs. Are you familiar with the new Church of the Saviour mission, World Peacemakers?"

"No, I've been so caught up in my recovery that I haven't been paying close attention to what's going on at church lately."

"It's a mission that was called into being by Bill Price. Their goal is to help small groups gather over the world to pray and advocate for peace and justice. Mary Lee Barker supported it with a grant so that they have the funding to set up an office on the third floor of Church of the Saviour headquarters. They are looking for a secretary to help them type up their newsletter and other publications. You could have to learn to use a computer for word processing—do you think you could learn to do that?"

"I've used computers for the National Jogging Association. It was frustrating at times, but maybe the technology has gotten better. Someday I want to be a creative writer, and it would be a real plus to know how to do word processing."

"They would also need you to balance their corporate checkbook. Do you think you could do that?"

"I've never balanced my own checkbook. I practice 'PMS banking'— at the end of the month, I just don't spend money. But I could learn. Would they give me a calculator?"

"I'm sure they would. Do you want to give it a try? I could send you out on an interview."

I nodded my head and said an enthusiastic, "Yes!"

The next morning, I took the bus from Porter Street to Church of the Saviour headquarters, where the World Peacemaker office was located. The friendly receptionist in the church office pointed me up the stairs to the third floor. I knew that part of the building well because I had played there as a child and slid down the banisters. Even before I knocked on the office door of Director Bill Price, something told me that this was where I belonged.

Bill Price was a grandfatherly man with thick, wild gray hair. He had something in common with my maternal grandfather—he was a retired physicist. He was familiar with a textbook my grandfather, Thomas B. Brown, had written, called *Brown's Physics*. Bill was deeply committed to peacemaking and preventing nuclear war.

He asked me if I was familiar with the sentence in the Church of the Saviour mission statement that all members are challenged to recommit to yearly: "I will seek to be loving in all relations with other individuals, groups, classes, races, and nations and will seek to be a reconciler, living in a manner which will end all war, personal and public."

"Yes, I've always been moved by that," I said. "Though I'm not a full church member." Membership in the Church of the Saviour was a lengthy and involved process, including taking classes in the School of Christian Living, writing a spiritual autobiography, joining a mission group, and committing to tithing.

To make a long story short, Bill offered me the job, I accepted it, and the job was a good fit for all my differently abled gifts. My patient coworker Fern Edwards trained me on using a personal computer. I got to transcribe dictation from writer Henri Nouwen. With flexible hours, I worked faithfully even on mornings when I overslept. I learned how to balance the office checkbook using a manual calculator with a crank handle. Best of all, my coworkers met for prayer and meditation every Monday morning.

P.J. O'Rourke once said, "Everybody wants to save the earth; nobody wants to help Mom do the dishes." Being secretary at World Peace-makers was both a lofty vocation and a practical way of making a difference in the world. When I was given keys to the office, it was like having the keys to a castle. I was truly dwelling in the house of the Lord.

Chapter 11

The Key of Three Wise Women and the Gifts They Brought

As I continue writing this story, I have been celebrating Christmas and Epiphany. Hearing the familiar story of how the three magi brought their gifts to the Christ Child, I giggled a bit, imagining how things might have gone differently if the three "wise men" had been "wise women." Perhaps they might have brought practical gifts like diapers, comforters, and chicken soup.

I was blessed by the gifts of three such wise women in the early 1980s. As I regained my mental health, I joined a Seeker's Community Mission Group called "Learners and Teachers." The group's mission included sponsoring a Wednesday evening gathering called "The School of Christian Living." There were core classes required for membership, such as "Old Testament," "New Testament," and "Christian Community." There were also electives like "Christian Clowning." Our inward calling included daily prayer and Bible study, writing reports for our group's spiritual director, and meeting weekly for several hours. The mission group became a huge support for me, a place of belonging and affirmation, where I learned from the others and taught them from my wisdom of lived experience. Three mission group members played a key role in my healing journey: Ellen Griffith, Muriel Lipp, and Christine Weaver. We had a back-and-forth experience of teaching and learning from each other.

Ellen Griffith was a lawyer who worked for a group called *For Love of Children* (FLOC). They aimed to teach, empower, and transform children and youth in the Washington, D.C. area. It remains a respected nonprofit to this day. In addition to fiercely defending at-risk children, she was a compassionate advocate for homeless persons suffering from mental illness.

When I spoke openly to the mission group about my mental health struggles, Ellen spoke up about her own diagnosis of living with bipolar illness. She wanted to make it clear that no one should think of their illness as a "dark night of the soul" to simply endure and pray about. She stressed the importance of finding the right medication for the right diagnosis. She was under the care of psychiatric providers who called themselves "psychopharmacologists." She encouraged me to see them for a second opinion.

At this point, I had been diagnosed as having schizophrenia and was taking older, traditional antipsychotics with unpleasant side effects. These psychopharmacologists didn't ask questions about what my childhood was like or what the contents of my hallucinations might mean. Psychotherapy was not their approach; they stressed medication over talking therapy. After an intake interview and a trial of an MAOI antidepressant, they re-diagnosed me as bipolar and prescribed lithium.

Looking back, that was not an accurate diagnosis. My symptoms were more psychotic than mood related. And I did need to talk about them! Lithium didn't make me as numb and subdued as Haldol, but it had its own side effect challenges. In the years to follow, my diagnosis would change from bipolar to schizoaffective and finally to schizophrenia. By that point, there were newer, more effective medicines for schizophrenia with fewer side effects. Also, I gradually realized that there was a place for psychotherapy, provided it was cognitive therapy with practical support, not psychoanalysis probing trauma of the distant past.

Even so, Ellen gave me the gift of advocacy for better psychiatric health care and the insight that mental illness is a brain disorder, a chronic physical illness like diabetes. She helped me reject shame and embrace treatment informed by science. She also opened my eyes to the plight of mental illness experienced by people who are homeless. She taught me to understand they were not homeless by choice. Rather, their illness impaired their ability to make good choices. The stigma against them made obtaining housing, food, and health care harder. As a lawyer, Ellen worked with advocacy groups to fight for the dignity and human rights of these marginalized people, and she opened my eyes to see how easily we could have been in their shoes.

A second woman in "Learners and Teachers" was Muriel Lipp. I knew Muriel from childhood as she and her family attended Church of the Saviour. She had four children. Eddie, her son, was the oldest and she had three daughters. Her middle daughter, Kathy, was my age. We'd been in the church teen youth group together. One Saturday a month, we waitressed together at the Potter's House Coffee Shop. I would go home with Kathy afterward and stay overnight at her house, getting a ride to church in the morning. As a teenager, I returned to being called Margaret at school because my teachers insisted I couldn't use my nickname; many of my peers didn't catch on to the nickname either. But when I was at Kathy's house, her mom remembered to call me Margalea and it felt so right and true to my real self. It was one of the reasons I started asking others to call me Margalea as well, and I now use it almost exclusively except at the bank and the doctor's office.

By now, I was in my early twenties. Having Muriel in my mission group made her feel more like a peer than a friend's mom. We had in common that we were both writers beginning to be published. She was the group's spiritual director, so she read my weekly written reports on how I was keeping my spiritual discipline. Her feedback was warm and encouraging. I felt heard and affirmed.

On May 2, 1982, Muriel tragically lost her son Eddie to suicide. I grieved with her and for her. It opened a door in my heart to understand how much my mother would suffer if I took my life. Muriel told me it helped her to hear from me what I was thinking and feeling when I had previously attempted suicide. She lived in Virginia, and she would walk beside the Potomac River every morning, wailing her grieving prayers to God.

I've recently gotten back in touch with Kathy and saw her in person last summer. By now, we've both lost our parents. I asked her about Muriel's grief for Eddie. She said, "I remember two things that were helpful to Mom. She chose a hymn for the funeral: *There is a Balm in Gilead*. And she loved a poem by Rilke about accepting all that is unsolved in your heart. Live into the questions themselves; love the questions until you live into the answer."

Kathy said, "Mom and Dad talked about you often and updated me on your visits. They were so inspired by your ability to overcome the challenges of brain illness and live such a full life. I think your example gave them so much help for other people."

Christine Weaver was the third wise woman who came into my life during this critical time. She was in her late sixties and had come to Washington, D.C. from Goshen, Indiana, to serve as head of the Nutrition Department at Howard University for a year, helping them to improve their program and become accredited. She had special empathy for students of color who'd been challenged by poverty and stigma. She had lived through the Great Depression and survived because her family could harvest a big garden, storing food in canning jars and a root cellar. Besides economic depression, she had a depression of spirit and dropped out of high school because she had little self-esteem. She took a job as a housekeeper and childcare provider for a physician and his family. The doctor recognized that Christine was intelligent and deserved a college education. He mentored her and paid her way to Goshen College. It was a huge challenge, especially chemistry class, but she didn't give up. She went on to get her master's and later her Ph.D. She rose in academia and was head of the Nutrition Program at the University of Missouri.

Christine was an overcomer, for sure! The more I heard her story, the more I hoped to be like her. After Eddie's death, Muriel asked Christine to take on the role of the mission group's spiritual director, as Muriel needed respite to grieve the tragedy. Christine read my weekly reports and said they demonstrated that I was a good writer. We met at the Potter's House to talk about it. She asked me if I had ever considered applying to the University of Iowa's Writer's Workshop. She had done graduate studies at the University of Iowa, loved Iowa City, and made life-long friendships in the community. I said I would think it over.

The other important conversation Christine and I had was about whether I should consider adult baptism. Christine was a Mennonite, and Mennonites are part of the Anabaptist tradition of adult baptism. Mennonites believed so strongly in this that they endured prison and horrible executions for their faith. It is part of their identity as peacemakers. For me, it seemed like a path to peacemaking. Later, I met with Seekers Church pastors Sonya Dyer and Fred Taylor, and we discussed and planned my baptism.

These three wise women offered me the gifts of wisdom and hope. I wasn't just a passive receiver; I worked hard to embrace their gifts. They affirmed that I had taught them and inspired them as well. It was as if a heavenly dance coach led us in a waltz, counting out "one, two, three."

Chapter 12

The Key of Baptism in a Muddy Lake

The clear blue sky made the muddy waters of the Lake of the Saints at Dayspring Retreat Farms sparkle. I was being baptized to make an adult affirmation of faith. I was pledging to turn away from self-hatred and self-harm. I was asking to be cleansed of the sin of judging myself and other people. My best friend since junior high, Martha, who'd had my back when my brain was on fire, opened the scriptures to me regarding adult baptism. I knew life could and would get messy, just like the muddy waters that I was going to be immersed in. That's why I wore white painter's pants instead of a fancy white dress.

I was reminded that just a year and a half ago, I had come close to ending my life in the muddy, polluted waters of the Potomac River. I had been listening to "the voices." I suspected I had not heard the last of "the voices," but I was committing to no longer obeying them, not giving them the power to destroy me.

It reminds me of how Jesus used mud to heal the eyes of the blind man and how Jesus affirmed that his blindness was not caused by the sin of the man or his parents. Like the healed man, I knew it was

Christ who healed me, and I was determined to be Jesus' follower even if I had to face the stigma of a society that wanted to shame me for having a broken brain.

My family and friends sat down on the grassy banks of the lake, and Paster Sonya opened in prayer. We sang "Amazing Grace" in English, and then I sang it in French. I learned to sing it in French when I was a college student in Paris and later in Quebec City. It reminded me of disciples being empowered to speak in ways everyone could understand. Then I was invited to wade into the lake accompanied by two pastors. The coolness of the water felt good in the heat of the day. We stopped when the water was waist high. "Margalea," said Pastor Fred, "we are going to lower you down into the water of death and raise you up into life. Remember to pinch your nose." With Pastor Fred on my left and Pastor Sonya on my right, I let my weight rest in the grip of their hands. Down, down, down into muddy water. Up, up, up into light and life.

As I came up, I had a vision of turning a key into a locked door and having it swing open wide. Light shone through.

Back on the shore of the lake, a Christian clown, Ellen Griffith, gave me a hug, both of us covered in mud. She teased me to smell her flower, which squirted me in the face with water. Holy laughter! New beginnings! Choosing life!

Chapter 13

From Victim to Survivor and the Messy In-Between

On the evening of November 20, 1983, my housemate Alfred drove me to a friend's house in the Northwest Washington, D.C., neighborhood to watch a television film about nuclear war. We didn't have a television in our house, and this film seemed important to watch as persons committed to peacemaking. The movie was called "The Day After," about what the consequences would be if a fictional war between the NATO forces and the Warsaw Pact that escalated into a full-scale nuclear attack. It was grim to watch. About an hour into it, I'd had my fill. I asked Alfred for a ride home, but he wanted to stay for the rest of the movie. We weren't very far from our house, and I knew I could catch a bus if I walked a few blocks. But when I got outside, I realized it was dark and rainy, and I almost changed my mind. But I decided my need to get away from the gruesome movie outweighed the risks of going home solo.

I briskly walked the few blocks to the bus stop. I felt uneasy but reminded myself this was a safe neighborhood. I boarded the bus and sat toward the back. I wish I had sat closer to the driver. My heart started beating faster when I noticed that the night route Metrobus took a different turn, and instead of stopping outside my house, it turned into a condominium complex. I knew if I didn't get off here, the bus would go further and further away from home. Trees surrounded the condominium buildings and there was no way anyone could see me get off the bus. There were old-fashioned lamp posts, but they provided only dim lighting.

I took a deep breath and got off the bus through the back door. The bus roared away. Somehow, my peripheral vision told me that someone got off the bus right behind me. I started to run, using all the strength I had built up working for the National Jogging Association. But only a few yards later, strong arms grabbed my shoulders and pulled me down from behind. I landed on my back in the wet grass. He flipped my legs in the air, pulled down my jogging pants, and raped me anally. It was painful and violating. I was unable to breathe, unable to scream. Even if I had screamed, there was no one to hear me or save me. It seemed to last hours but was probably only a few minutes. He tossed my purse to my side, took nothing from it, and ran away.

I don't know why, but I whispered to him, "I forgive you." Why? Why? I hated him. I wanted to kill him. I wanted him to be violated the way he had violated me. Somehow, the words came out of my mouth. I think I said it more for my sake than his. I can understand if my reader doesn't believe me. It's hard to believe myself, but I know I did say it.

I crawled to my hands and knees and slowly stood. I pulled my jogging pants back up. I limped the two blocks home. I came inside the house and walked upstairs to knock on the door of my housemate, Mary. I told her what happened through sobs. She embraced me and shared her own story of date rape years before. She urged me to call the police and be seen by a doctor, but I just wasn't ready to do that. I wanted to take a tub bath and wash away the violation. I hoped I could somehow sleep away the nightmare.

The next day, I went to the Church of the Saviour clinic on Columbia Road. Dr. Janelle Goetcheus examined me. The bath I had taken the night before had removed much of the evidence, but she did find pieces of grass in my anus. She didn't do a pregnancy test because the rape was anal. She said she was so very sad about what I had endured. She praised me for my courage and resilience. She urged me to report the rape to the police so that other women might be protected from the predator. I later did so, but I could not provide any detail of the rapist's appearance because he was so much in the shadow.

Dr. Goetcheus had me meet with one of their clinic nurses. The nurse told me that she had been raped a few months ago while walking home from the clinic. She sat and talked with me, and we both cried. She had written a paraphrase of the 23rd Psalm, and she asked me if I would like to read it. I said yes, I would very much like that. I read and reread it, keeping it in my wallet for years before I somehow misplaced it. By then, I had internalized it.

This is how I would express it decades later:

> The Lord is my shepherd, always walking with me, and I will never lack a presence of tender, protecting love.

> He restores the dignity of my person and body, leading me beside the still waters of recovered calm.

> Yes, though I walk through the shadow of death, the shadow of violation, the shadow of hateful violence, I will fear no evil because my enemy has no power to destroy my soul or break my spirit.

> You prepare a table of nourishing comfort in the presence of enemy voices who lie to me that the rape wasn't rape or that it was my fault for being a single woman walking alone.

> You anoint me with the oil of self-compassion; my cup of self-esteem is full and running over.

Instead of the terror of my attacker chasing me, goodness and mercy will gently pursue me and I will dwell in the shelter of being your beloved, beautiful daughter forever.

Like the psalmists often do, I didn't hold back from God my raw emotions. I cried out: "Jesus, why did you let this happen to me? Why did you let that man violate me? Why don't you punish him?" I vividly imagined how I would have liked to have him punished. But then I took a deep breath. The screams I couldn't scream during the attack were released. Someone *did* hear my screams! Someone came to me, helping me survive the ordeal physically, mentally, and spiritually. That someone was Jesus.

I don't want to minimize the trauma; I was haunted by flashbacks. I thought the rapist followed me even when I moved from Washington, D.C., to Iowa, a thousand miles away. Because all I saw of the rapist in the dim light was his dark skin, I had to ask for my heart to be cleansed of racism to not see all men of color as dangerous. This key of prayer let light into the broken places, and I now have wonderful male and female friends of color, which has been a huge help in cleansing my heart of this fear.

Chapter 14

The Key of Brave

Claiming each day as the first day of the rest of my life takes courage, and courage was something that my mentor Christine Weaver had a gift for evoking in me. By 1984, Christine had finished her time at Howard University and returned to her retirement home in Goshen, Indiana. We kept in touch by mail and phone calls. She persisted in encouraging me to come to Iowa City and explore the Writer's Workshop. Christine had done graduate studies in nutrition at the University of Iowa in the 1950s, had lived in a Mennonite household, and she still had close ties with friends in Iowa City. She stressed it was a safe city to live in, with little crime. She knew about the sexual assault I'd experienced and how much I valued safety.

In early May 1984, I decided to follow Christine's nudging. In my community household, we had just one common phone in the hallway. We had to write down each long-distance call we made so we could pay for them when the bill came. I wrote down the day and time. I dialed Christine's number and listened to the phone ring, my heart pounding.

Christine answered the phone, "Hello," and I could hear the warmth in her voice. This was long before caller ID. She didn't know it was me calling until I told her who I was. She was that welcoming of any phone call. It was part of how she was a good spiritual director to me and others.

"Christine," I said, "I think I'm ready to do it. I'm going to visit Iowa City. I can't afford airfare, but I can take the bus. Can I stop at your place on the way? Can you ask your friends in Iowa City to let me stay with them for a week while I check everything out?"

"Of course, I can do that!" Christine said. "This will be a decision you won't regret. I'll be praying for you to have traveling mercies."

The slang for Greyhound is "the dog." It's not the classiest form of transportation. Maybe they call it that because dogs, in general, are less snotty than cats and friendly to everyone they meet. I admire dogs' courage and how they defend their humans when perceiving danger. Cats are also that way, just more subtle. C.S. Lewis' Aslan comes to mind, a lion who isn't tame or safe but infinitely good. It took fierce animal courage for me to climb the steep three steps into the bus, carrying a backpack heavy with books, and sit down in the seat nearest the window. I closed my eyes and prayed, "God, please be with me."

The "dog" hauled me from Washington, D.C., to Pittsburgh, where my college friend Chris Enzerra picked me up and drove us to Bethany College campus in West Virginia to stay in one of the dorms overnight. The next morning, she drove me to her brother's home in Ohio. After staying overnight with her brother, I got back on the "dog" to go to Goshen, Indiana, where Christine lived. There was one small problem: the bus doesn't have an official stop in Goshen. But when I told the driver that was where I needed to go, he said that he did cross a railroad track in Goshen where he was required to stop and he could open the bus doors to let me jump off. I made that my plan.

I pretty much ignored the scenery as I rode along because my mind was focused on the books I had brought with me. I was especially drawn to an anthology of women writers, particularly an essay by Alice Walker titled *In Search of Our Mothers' Gardens*. Alice Walker saw her mother's flower garden as a symbol of her mother's strength, courage, creativity, and love at a time when women in general, especially women of color, had few creative outlets to pour their passions and creativity into. I reflected on my mother's creativity in sewing, drafting, painting, and journal writing. I wondered what my creative garden would look like if I moved to Iowa City. Could I possibly be accepted into the Writer's Work-shop? Would I meet others like me who were struggling to find a creative way to bring order out of chaos in our thinking? Would I go broke trying to live independently? Would Iowa City be as safe as Christine said it was?

Suddenly, the bus driver's voice startled me out of my musings. He shouted, "Goshen!" I got my suitcase down from the rack and put my backpack over my shoulder. I walked to the back door, which opened with a hiss, and jumped out. Goshen was where Goshen College was located, but the bus didn't drop me off on campus. I was in a suburban neighborhood; found my way to a convenience store. I assumed that if Goshen College was as close a community as Bethany College, where I did my undergrad, everyone would know everyone. Christine had been a student here and still interacted with college students in her retirement, especially international Asian students. She remembered food and culture from her missionary time in China and loved to have students gather in her home to cook and eat together. So, I fully expected the convenience store clerk to tell me where she lived.

"Christine who?" the young man replied.

"Weaver. W-E-A-V-E-R." I spelled it slowly in case he was a little illiterate.

I dug into my backpack for my address book and read him her address.

"Oh, yeah, you want to go to Greencroft Retirement center. Go down the highway and turn on a gravel road. It's about a mile."

A mile! This was late May and the heat was oppressive. I figured I'd need something cold to cool me off.

"How much is a soda?" I asked the clerk.

"Soda? Do you mean pop?"

I started to giggle. Only a county bumpkin would call a soft drink soda pop.

"Whatever you call it, I'd like to buy some."

I bought it and went out the door. I was a seasoned walker and didn't think a mile would take me that long. But the gravel road was challenging because my shoes kept grinding through it. The backpack full of books I had thought so essential to bring made my shoulders and back ache. The suitcase in my left hand felt like it would pull my arm off. What to do?

"Run!" the voices said. "You'll get there faster, and you can drop the bags at Christine's door."

I hadn't yet learned the wisdom of telling the voices no. So, I obeyed them. I had only run about fifty feet when I stumbled and fell forward. The breath knocked out of me. I felt like sticky yogurt was oozing from my knees, but I looked down and saw it was blood. I crawled onto hands and knees and slowly, stiffly, stood up. I heard a car motor coming up beside me, then stopping. It was a black car with black bumpers. A woman on the passenger side rolled down the window.

"You look like you're hurt. Are you okay? Can we give you a ride?"

She was wearing a funny white lace hat on the back of her head. As odd as that was, she wasn't scary. She seemed genuinely kind. My mother had told me never to hitchhike, but I badly needed a ride.

"Could you take me to Greencroft to see Christine Weaver? Maybe you know her?"

"We know some Weavers, but I'm not sure we know Christine. But we'd be happy to take you to Greencroft."

I got in the back seat of the car. I saw that the driver also had a funny little snowflake hat. Could this be a religious thing? Christine was a Mennonite, but I had never seen her wear one. In a few minutes, we were at the main Greencroft building. The ladies told me to go inside and get directions, and they would take me to whatever building Christine was in. Greencroft was a retirement community with various levels of care, from nursing home to apartments to cottages. Being a healthy young, late sixty-something, Christine lived in one of the cottages. I returned to the black car, and the ladies took me to a courtyard with a circle of five cottages.

"Thank you," I called out to the ladies. "This is it! Are you sure you don't know Christine? She's a Mennonite."

The driver said, "You're most welcome!" She seemed to suppress a laugh. I didn't yet know that this whole area of Indiana had a large population of Mennonites, so many that they jokingly called themselves a "Menno Ghetto."

I knocked on the door, and Christine opened it. It had been half a year since I had seen her but she was the same Christine with piercing blue eyes and white-grey hair pulled back into a bun.

"Oh, Margalea, it's so good to see you. But what has happened to you? You're all bloody! Come inside, and let us clean you up."

Another woman who looked like an older version of Christine was also in the cottage. She introduced herself as Christine's sister,

Dorothy, a retired nurse. They walked me into the bathroom, and Dorothy gently cleaned and bandaged my wounds. Years later, when I returned to visit Christine and Dorothy, Dorothy always remembered me as "the girl with the bloody knees."

Christine wanted me to meet with a friend and colleague who had graduated from the University of Iowa Writer's Workshop. I really missed out on an opportunity because of my fear that my writing wouldn't be good enough. Instead of coming directly to the appointment she'd made for us, I idled at the campus snack bar, buying a candy bar and a can of soda—okay, pop. I was ten or fifteen minutes late. I hadn't brought any of my writing with me to show him. I remember little about our meeting. I'm so sad looking back that I didn't challenge my unfounded thinking that I didn't have promise as a poet or essayist. I would have to allow myself to grow as a human being and a writer in order to stop sabotaging myself.

I stayed a few days in Goshen with Christine, and then she put me back on the bus to Iowa City, having called her friend Bob Summers to meet me at the bus station. She probably had to take me to another town to catch the bus because it wasn't like I could jump onto the bus at the railroad track. I remember big highway signs announcing we were going through "the Quad Cities," and then we went through more rural areas. The bus pulled into the Iowa City bus station at about five that evening. I noticed a brick wall with painted lettering saying, "Wilson's Sporting Goods." Below it was a drawing of a fish, an early Christian symbol. I read into that symbol that Iowa City was the place God wanted me to be.

Christine must have described me to Bob, and maybe my bandaged knees were a clue, because he greeted me with a cheerful, "You must be Margalea." He took me to his home, where his wife, Edith, introduced herself and explained that two of their daughters were away at music camp but that their oldest daughter, Kristine, was eager to meet me. After supper, I went to Kristine's room, and we had a good conversation. She showed me a picture of her fiancé, Tim Stalter. She shared her own story of recovery. I felt closer to the Summers family from that time on.

I stayed with the Summers for a week. I explored the city by bus and on foot. As a non-driver, I knew I had to have public transportation anywhere I lived. I walked on the sidewalks beside the Iowa River and enjoyed the flowering trees on its banks. I was awed by the University of Iowa Hancher Auditorium; it reminded me of the Washington, D.C., Kennedy Center. Iowa City had all the charm of Washington, D.C., but on a smaller scale. I put in my application to be considered for University of Iowa employment and used Bob Summers, who was a doctor at University Hospitals, as a reference. I found half a duplex house to rent from Mennonite landlords named the Zooks. Two months later, on August 1, I arrived in Iowa City, brought by my parents in a rented station wagon with my bicycle on the roof.

I will always be grateful that my parents had the courage and grace to let me move halfway across the country by myself, to forge my path in a whole new chapter of my life. I will never forget the wisdom Christine had in mentoring me. Christine and Dorothy bandaged up my wounded knees, but God mended my wounded spirit by bringing me here. And that amazing Hancher auditorium on the river? Thirty-eight years later, a ballet would be performed there, one that I would help inspire.

Chapter 15

The Key of Loving Your Iowa Neighbor as Yourself

I came to Iowa as a stranger in a strange land. I was strange indeed, as a person living with mental illness who was not yet well diagnosed and treated. I was an East Coast girl wearing a "mask" to keep my distance for safety. I was single and had never had a real romantic relationship. I was an ecumenical Christian and new to Mennonites. I was a nondriver used to riding the D.C. Metro subway, my face shielded by the Washington Post. But I was about to have all that melt in the warmth of Iowa nice.

My entrance into the Iowa City community was through the Summers family and with the First Mennonite Church of Iowa City, where they brought me to worship. It was a bit confusing that all these people had the same last name of Yoder, Gingerich, Miller, or even that tongue twister Swartzendruber. I later learned this was playing the Mennonite name game. It was a bit tribal. I introduced myself to one of the senior members as Margalea Warner, who paused and said, perplexed, "I don't think I know any Warners." Once we got past that awkwardness, I started feeling more like a distant cousin. One young adult woman named Joy Sutter welcomed

me into a young adult Sunday School class who had named themselves the "Menno-morphosis class," an image that we were being
transformed as Christians, as maturing adults, and as members of the
church and the larger community. The Menno part of the class name
was for Mennonites. Mennonites got their name from a Swiss
German leader named Menno Simons, and they didn't want to be
known as Simonites, so they went with Mennonites.

I found that about six senior church members knew my mentor
Christine Weaver from when she lived and studied here in the '50's.
They were gracious, funny, and just had good common sense. When
I didn't go to the Menno-morphosis class, I went to their class, Brud-
erschaft, a German word for *brotherhood*.

An important relationship that would last for over 40 years was with
a nurse in her late twenties named Marnetta Shetler Bradford. She
introduced herself to me the first Sunday after I moved there as living
in the duplex house next door to my duplex house. She welcomed me
to stop by any time and meet her housemates Coleen Kliewer and
Hope Nisly. Coleen was also a nurse and had served as a volunteer
with the Mennonite Central Committee with Marnetta in Brazil.
Hope was an undergraduate majoring in Women's Studies at the
University of Iowa. Marnetta also said she would happily give me a
ride to church. She carried through with that offer even when it
meant pounding on the door to find me still in my pajamas and
persisting in waiting until I was dressed (she said informal blue jeans
and a t-shirt would be fine) and gently pushing me out the door to
the car.

Outside church, I first met the family in the other half of the duplex I
rented. Their six-year-old daughter came by and stared in the living
room window.

She yelled through the open window, "Why do you have a bicycle
instead of a sofa?"

It seemed a little intrusive but I figured I could explain. "Because I came from a thousand miles away and traveled light. I'm too broke to buy a sofa. But I'm looking for housemates, and surely one of them will have furniture."

I later met her parents and learned her dad was a Baptist pastor.

My next experience of Iowa Nice neighbors were the folks I met riding the Iowa City buses. If the Greyhound bus was "the dog," I'd say these buses were a friendly mutt who greeted everyone by jumping up and giving them a big, sloppy dog kiss.

The driver said, "Good morning," and seemed to expect a "Good morning" in return. The other passengers made eye contact even if it meant looking up from their newspapers. A woman with a slight speech impediment introduced herself as Melody and asked me what my name was. I had the grace not to say, "It's none of your business." Over time, I learned other names, including the name of the driver, Jeff. One time, a passenger brought a Tupperware dish of frosted cupcakes and offered them to us, saying, "It's Jeff's birthday."

The next neighbors were my boss and coworkers at the University of Iowa research lab at the VA Hospital. My boss was Dr. Phil Schmid, who took a chance on me because he knew Bob and Edith Summers and believed in me even though he suspected something might be a little off. The lab supervisor, Don Lund, had a calm and steady manner and said I could come to him with any questions. Research Assistant Alberto Subieta greeted me every morning with a loud and enthusiastic, "Good morning, how are you?" and listened for an answer in a way I could not refuse.

Over the following years, I became vulnerable with these neighbors in a risky way. I felt ashamed sometimes for doing so, but God didn't let me stay stuck in shame. I felt they were Good Samaritans; they did not pass by on the other side.

Remember, I was not yet diagnosed with schizophrenia, and the medicines I was on for bipolar really weren't working. I was bewildered to be hearing vicious voices and unarmed with keys for self-defense. Those keys would come, but not yet. I couldn't go around my illness; I had to go through.

One night, after I had found two wonderful housemates that I felt safe with, I heard voices that were threatening to devour me. I knew it wasn't housemates Carla or Becky. It had to be coming through the duplex wall. I went outside my bedroom door, out the duplex door, and pounded on the neighbor's door. Fortunately, I was wearing a nightgown and not in my underwear.

The father opened the door and said, "Margalea, what's wrong?"

"I need you to stop calling me a whore. I am not a bad person. I can't sleep with all your yelling. Please make all the voices stop. They told me you can make it stop."

"I'm not sure I can help you. I promise we were asleep and not yelling at you. Would it help if we sat with you and prayed?"

"What makes you so kind? Oh please, please try to pray with me."

We sat on his sofa (they didn't just have a bicycle), and he asked permission to hold my hand. I have no memory of what words he prayed, but they turned the volume of the voices from loud to low static background. They could have reported me to the police for harassment but something or Someone gave them the grace not to do that.

My work, family, and neighbors asked, "How are you?" and heard my, "Not very good." They taught me how to overcome the demons of technology. They celebrated my birthday after asking what celebration I wanted, if any. They prevented suicide attempts by stopping me from wading into the Iowa River (they followed me out the door of the hospital and ran after me once) and escorted me to the hospital ER. They held my job while I was in the hospital. I'm not sure I would have had the grace to do that if I had been their coworker. It was Iowa Nice on loudspeaker. I even suspect it was Iowa Love.

But the neighbor who was most neighborly in the deepest way was Marnetta. She set a place at her table when I was almost broke and couldn't afford food beyond cornflakes and instant coffee. She was a downright bossy neighbor sometimes, coming to give me a ride to church saying, "Margalea, you need Jesus more than you need to go back to bed." She continued to be my neighbor when I moved to other homes in Iowa City.

On a Sunday morning when I didn't come out for her ride, she knew in the pit of her stomach that I was in grave danger. Seeing the door was locked, she broke in through the screen window. Finding me unconscious, she called 911. The rest is a long, long story, but she fought off the bandit illness that had attacked me, bandaged my physical and mental wounds, and found me a better psychiatrist when the current one wanted to admit me long-term to a state hospital. When she moved to another state, she found a visiting counseling group that helped me problem-solve crises and taught me life skills like budgeting, balancing my checkbook, and goal setting. Marnetta's long-term care for me was like the Good Samaritan paying the Innkeeper to tend to the trauma survivor while the Samaritan had to be away.

Decades later, I was given the gift of walking beside Marnetta when she encountered mental illness in her family and started seeing a therapist for her own self-care. Her friendship not only saved my life but made my life richer and more whole. Now that I am not experiencing crisis after crisis, it feels like a balanced friendship of mutual support.

At one crisis point, I asked my mother, "Can I move back in with you?"

She said gently and firmly, "No, Margalea. Iowa is your home now. I've been there, and I know your neighbors. They love you as much or more than I do. I trust them to keep you safe."

I write this chapter from a place of health and recovery, but the voices still find a way to hiss at me sometimes. "How could you be such a weak, spineless, stupid, childish, crazy girl to move away from home and expect strangers to take care of you?"

I follow the string of that thought and question its truth: What is weak about making a whole new start in a new community? How am I standing so tall if I don't have a spine? What is stupid—or foolish—about trusting kindness when you receive it? What is crazy about overcoming mental health challenges?

I speak to myself as a friend would, saying, "You have loved your Iowa neighbor as yourself. Keep reciprocating the kindness."

Chapter 16

The Key to the Quiet Room

When I was first admitted to University Hospitals for a psychiatric crisis in the mid-1980s, I was alarmed by the prison-like fortress I was entering. The building was built in 1919 with thick brick walls and small barred windows. The sign outside it could not have been more stigmatizing: *University of Iowa Psychopathic Hospital*. Now, I understand that psychopathic is a legitimate medical word with a root meaning of *mind disorder*. But popular culture hears the word psychopathic and thinks of crazies with knives slashing sexy young women in the shower. I had been in locked wards in other hospitals, but something about this grim fortress made for the sole purpose of locking up people like me made me recoil. In years to come, I would have frequent stays there, and it felt more like a prison every time.

One morning, I woke up in the psychopathic hospital with a bad headache. I had been up multiple times in the night to scribble in my notebook in the dim light about the visions I'd been having. But now, looking through the pages, I realized I could not read my own handwriting. Some of the meds I was on caused my handwriting to be shaky, but I blamed my own ineptitude. I ran my hand through my tangled hair. I heard the chattering voices of doctors coming down the hall to make rounds.

"How did you sleep, Margaret?" Dr. A. asked.

Why did they always ask that when it was their fault that they woke you up from what little sleep you got?

"I didn't sleep because I was up in the night writing. Have you read the poem I asked the nurse to put in my chart? I think it has a clue to what will make me better."

"Margaret," Dr. A. snapped back, "I'm a busy man. If I took time to read your psychotic scribblings, I wouldn't have time to write research papers."

I only hoped the scientific journal editors had the same opinion of Dr A.'s writing as he had of mine.

I raised my voice, saying, "This medicine you're giving me is poison. I can't think or feel anything when I take it. I'm not going to take it anymore."

Dr. A.'s face and neck flushed red. His eyes seemed to bulge.

"You are the most non-compliant patient I've ever had the misfortune of being assigned. I'm seriously considering committing you to the state hospital."

A scream came out of my mouth, and I watched it rise in a tall flame. I pulled on the drawer handle of my wooden dresser beside me. I yanked the whole thing off its grooves. With my bare hands, I pulled and twisted the cheap fiberboard wood of the drawer until it broke apart. The splinters scratched my hands, and I bled.

The staff doctor shouted to the PNAs (Psychiatric Nurse Assistants), "Take this female to the QR (Quiet Room) and restrain her."

Two strong men grabbed my arms and dragged me out of the room, down the hall, and into the QR. I bit one of them in the leg and got a mouthful of leg hair, which I spit out. The PNAs told me to change out of my street clothes and into a hospital gown. I was wearing a button-down shirt. I ripped it open without unbuttoning it, sending buttons flying like hail, bouncing across the concrete floor. There was more yanking and lifting me onto a hard metal bed. Leather straps were buckled around my torso, arms, and lower legs. I heard the door slam shut and the clicking of a key. What was the point of locking the door when I was already trapped in these restraints like a fly in a spider's web? I was afraid the restraining belts might squeeze the breath right out of me.

I took a shallow breath—I could still breathe—and exhaled in a bellow—a roar. I was determined not to let the Quiet Room silence me. I had heard other patients screaming in seclusion, so the Quiet Room was a misnomer. It was the loud room, the rebel room.

There was a fan in the ceiling above me. The voices love to turn mechanical sounds into words that growl. Words that lie. Words that molest.

"Die, girl! We won't shut up until you shut your mouth forever. That doctor was right; you're not ever going to get better. High functioning? You can't even function well enough to write with legible handwriting. Writer? You're not a writer. You steal words from us, and we can take them right back. You pretend to be sick to get attention. You aren't sick, but you sure are dying. You're not going to die in hospice, either. No nurses will manage your pain. No family will be at your bedside as you die. You'll be surrounded by hate."

I squirmed around in my restraints. I needed to pee. I was not going to use a bedpan.

That mindful moment of discomfort turned down the voices' volume a bit.

They vibrated instead of yelling. "Don't you even try to ask God to rescue you. God doesn't exist. God has hated you since the day you were born."

Wait a minute, If God doesn't exist, how can God hate me? I may be crazy, but I'm not stupid. What other lies could they be telling me? The voice's gossipy attack reminded me of the song, "Pick a little, talk a little, cheep, cheep, cheep, talk a lot, pick a little more."

I asked more questions. "Could I really deserve to be hated by God? Or by anyone else? Even if I committed bloody murder (something I had just attempted to do to that hateful doctor), could I deserve the death penalty? I had acted out to get attention, but didn't I deserve some attention?"

I prayed a one-word prayer: Help. That was a good enough prayer. I was a good enough person. I mean a really, really good enough person. I based that belief not on anything I had accomplished so far, even though I had accomplished a lot, but on my value as a body and soul with breath.

I was gonna bust out of these restraints. I was gonna open that locked door from the inside. I was gonna reach out and grab a fistful of keys to get me out of all the doors that had tried to contain me.

After what seemed like a century, but may have been just an hour, one of the PNAs named Eric opened the door.

Eric said, "The doctor says it's time to take you out of restraints and seclusion. Will you promise me you're done acting out?"

"Yes," I said, "and I'm sorry I bit you in the leg. It didn't taste good."

He chuckled. It always makes me feel better when somebody laughs at my jokes.

Eric unbuckled the leather straps that tethered me. My arms felt like they were floating up all by themselves. I turned on my side and slowly sat up.

"Come on," Eric said. "Let's get you out of here and back into proper clothes. I don't think you can wear that shirt you ripped off, though."

"No, I'm going to need a new one. I'm going to need a lot of new things from here on out."

That hour in the Quiet Room was the lowest lifetime bottom of a pit. A slimy pit. But what I learned there helped me climb out. My fierce will to live gave me a foothold. I cried out for the help I needed. This brings to mind a cartoon. A man who has fallen into a well calls out, "Lassie, get help!" Next frame: Lassie is pictured lying on her back on the therapist's couch. Like Lassie, I found I was allowed on some really comfy therapist's couches, provided I just asked them—and my insurance company—for their help. And my cries for help caused helpers to lower a rope to me, which I grabbed hold of with all my strength.

I did have times of sliding back down into the pit. Once, it rained so hard that I almost drowned there. That landmark of despair happened in August of 1993, after the greatest flooding in Iowa history. Virtually every maximum precipitation record was broken. I probably also broke records for the number of suicide attempts and most revolving door hospitalizations in just 34 years of staying alive. I was hospitalized after being rescued from trying to drown myself in the high waters of the Iowa River.

The difference this time was that I was part of a psych floor at the main hospital. I was under the kind care of Dr. Del Miller, a psychiatrist who was as humble as Dr. A. was arrogant. Instead of ordering me to comply, he invited me to commit to the risk of the adventure of life instead of death by self-hatred. He offered me a medicine called Clozapine, which is to this day considered the gold standard for schizophrenia. It is not usually the first medicine used because of its potentially fatal side effect of lowering immune response, which can lead to death by pneumonia. Dr. Miller said if I could tolerate it, Clozapine would help with both the "positive symptoms" of psychosis and the "negative symptoms" of numbness and lethargy. I welcomed what I hoped would be a chance to thrive. After my first dose, I perceived a deep stillness that I can only describe as shalom. By shalom, I mean peace that includes wholeness and completeness felt in body and mind. In the days that followed, as the dose was increased, the welcome silence of the voices grew larger and more spacious.

I was soon considered stable enough to participate in group activities outside the hospital, including riding in the hospital van to Coralville Lake. The flooding had exposed fossils dating back almost 200 million years, before the dinosaurs. I reached out to trace my fingers along the ridges of the fossils. How far back in time my suffering went! But my story was still moving forward.

After a week and a half, I was discharged and returned to full-time work and living independently. Two years later, I was put on a new medicine because the psychiatrist who followed me at the time thought it would be safer for my immune system. It was much less effective, and I relapsed, had another suicide attempt, and was hospitalized. Since discharge in June 1995, I've stayed true to my promise not to take my life. I've also done everything possible to keep from needing any more psych hospitalizations. I celebrate anniversaries of freedom by gathering with friends and adding to a collection of literal keys I display in a shadow box. By the grace of God, I hope to reach more anniversaries of recovery and freedom.

Once I sent my brain on an assignment to find keys, keys kept coming to me. In 2014, Dr. Todd Ingram, a professor of psychiatric nursing, heard my recovery story at a NAMI meeting. He then gave me the key to the Old Psych Hospital's Quiet Room. He said he captured it when the hospital closed and merged with the main hospital. When he handed the key to me, I was amazed by the size and weight of it. It was four inches by two and a half inches. It had a large letter A inside an oval. It felt cool to the touch. I have no doubt it is an antique and valuable to collectors. But it is of infinite value to me. I claim the key to the Quiet Room as an image of rebirth. Some resurrections take more than three days. Mine began in the Quiet Room, decades ago, and now I can't keep quiet about it.

Chapter 17

The Key of Joy in the Journey

I am writing this chapter from a writer's retreat called *Pen to Paradise* at the Richard Bush Renewal Retreat Center in Bannister, Michigan. It seemed like some negative force was trying to block me from getting here. Perhaps even trying to block my writing.

I've been working with story coach Marcy Pusey since January of 2023 and she's guided me in overcoming writer's block and beyond that, personal life block. I know I'm a good enough person regardless of anything I do or don't do. I have value as a child of God. Marcy has affirmed that I am a gifted writer. My motivation for coming on the retreat led by Marcy and Gary Williams was to have a time of accountability and focus to make progress on this memoir, *Dancer of Life*. I also know about myself that my style of creativity is to surround myself with community. In our strategy call earlier that week, I committed to writing strong and making progress on this memoir.

I faced obstacle after obstacle in the literal travel from Cedar Rapids, Iowa to Bannister, Michigan. I stayed in a hotel close to the airport because my flight was scheduled to leave at 5 a.m. My day of travel started at 3 a.m., when my body woke up even though the hotel wake-up call I'd requested never came. I enjoyed my friendly Lyft driver who took me from the hotel to the airport but wished I had arranged an earlier ride because the airport was swarmed with black-and-gold-wearing fans traveling to our Hawkeye women's basketball championship games. Demons of technology made it hard to print my boarding pass, but fellow passengers came to my aid. Then, my flight to Houston was delayed over two hours, and I couldn't make my connecting flight to Detroit. To add insult to injury, when we got to Houston, the pilot announced we would have to find a different gate because ours was blocked by bees. Bees? Bees!

Finally in Houston airport, I went to American Airlines customer service (I'm mentioning their name in case this published writing shames them into giving me a refund) and got another flight arranged, but one that was too late to meet up with a fellow writer friend as planned to drive the 121 miles to the retreat lodge. I had been texting Marcy impediment after impediment, and she helped me with problem-solving. She found a bus service that could take me, in two hours, to East Lansing Marriott for only $33. From there, I could get a Lyft ride.

Knowing things were going to work out to get me there no matter what, I went to Mc Donalds to use my $12 food voucher. I ordered a Happy Meal and a senior coffee. The clerk chuckled at the contradiction of my request.

He asked, "Do you want a bottle of water, too? You have to use the whole voucher in one place."

"Sure, I'll take water. And the toy. Don't forget the toy."

I sat down at the nearest gate. I plugged my phone into the outlet below the seat to charge because its battery was as low as my body and mind's battery was. I took the sandwich out of the Happy Meal box with the golden arch ears. Then the fries. And the apple slices. And at the very bottom, the toy.

Oh, boy! What was it? The box had a picture of a character who looked like the flexible toy of my childhood, Gumby. But it said he was Ron. And what did Ron's word balloon say?

"Just Dance."

Dance? Dance! Dance! Dance! All my weariness melted away. This memoir is titled

Choosing Dance Over Despair. This year of my life while I complete my memoir is powered by the mantra "keep dancing." I would have stood up and done a little happy dance if I wasn't afraid airport security would come and drag me away to their airport quiet room or jail. Instead of a body dance, I danced mentally by furiously scribbling in my notebook the next chapter of *Choosing Dance Over Despair*. I kept up my progress, scribbling away on my next flight.

Miracles continued: Smooth flight into Detroit and my bag was ready to grab. Strangers helped me find the bus "Michigan Flyer." I watched the sun set over beautiful clouds out the big bus windows. Arriving in East Lansing, I had a few moments of struggle with the Lyft app (only my second time ever using it), but within 15 minutes, Lyft driver Khrystyna arrived; I spotted her pale blue car and license plate. I could have hugged her, but she was already grabbing my suitcase and putting it in her trunk. She said she'd never been to the retreat center and that she lived in Detroit, but she had GPS that would get us there. The GPS robot voice said it should be a 49-minute ride.

I suspected by her accent and by the Cyrillic alphabet on her radio that she was international, but I couldn't guess for sure what country.

"Are you Russian?" I asked her.

"No. No. No. I'm Ukrainian. Russia is killing Ukraine. I fled the war in Ukraine 11 months ago with my daughter because I love my life and I love my daughter."

I was glad she didn't throw me out of the car for my stupidity in misunderstanding her nationality. We went on to have a delightful conversation despite some language barriers. I asked her if she was going to see the solar eclipse Monday and she said she had never heard of it but was sure GPS could get her there.

Marcy texted me that we should see the sign and the lighted building up the driveway beside it. By now it was quite dark. The driver spotted the sign saying, "Richard Bush Renewal Retreat Center" and I saw the bright lights of the building at the top of the driveway. Marcy was standing outside to greet me with open arms. Gary grabbed my suitcase and opened the door to let me in. I had started this trip at 3 a.m. and was arriving at my destination at 10 p.m.

I was home! My fellow writers, who had been following my progress as reported by Marcy, greeted me with a, "Go, Margalea!" cheer. More hugs, a hot meal, and I collapsed in my bed. I dreamed of flying through swarms of bees, or they could have been Iowa Hawkeye fans dressed in black and gold. When I awoke, I saw the note that I must have knocked off my bed in my hurry to get into it.

It was from Marcy, saying,

"You made it! God made a way! Miracle upon miracle! I can't wait to see your book DONE. It's going to impact so many lives. Love you so much! —Marcy."

And on the floor next to the note was a box I almost stumbled on. Among other treasures inside was a journal notebook with the title, "If you want to change the world, pick up your pen and write!"

I knew if I could overcome all the obstacles in my journey coming to the retreat in Bannister, Michigan, I could overcome anything that might block my creativity. I wouldn't be blocked by fear that I might not be good enough because this was a place where I was anchored in my value as a child of God with a story the world needed to hear. Not blocked by comparing myself to other writers because, surrounded by fellow creatives, I had the confidence to thrive and shine.

I set up my laptop Saturday morning at my own table between the tables of writers Elsie and Tina. We exchanged shouts of victory when we reached high points in our writing and exchanged hugs when writing about hard things. I wasn't blocked in writing about hard things because I knew I was in a safe place where I could direct my thoughts as if observing the trauma. I went on to write about what resurrection recovery looked like. My fellow writers affirmed me for how persistently I stayed with it. I didn't finish the whole book, but I completed three strong chapters, including this one, which I never knew was going to be in the book. My brain got the message loud and clear that I am unstoppable. I found joy in the journey, both the challenging day of travel to Bannister, Michigan, and the journey of growth as a person and a writer. I can keep choosing dance over despair.

Chapter 18

The Key of Being a Good Steward of the Gift of Story

I took a deep breath and looked around the circle of 17 medical students. My co-presenter and I were here to educate them about our mental health recovery journey and to help them better serve the patients they were seeing on their rotation through psychiatry. The students seemed like kids to me, them being their mid-twenties and me being almost 65. I caught myself thinking that they had to be so much smarter than I was and couldn't possibly learn from what I had to say. But I challenged that thought and reminded myself that I had the wisdom of lived experience and a story only I could tell. A verse I came across in my morning devotionals came to mind,

> *"Pray also for me, that whenever I speak, words may be given me so that I will fear-lessly make known the mystery of the gospel, for which I am an ambassador in chains. Pray that I may declare it fear-lessly, as I should."*

— Ephesians 6:19-20

Those words renewed my confidence and I boldly told my story.

I opened with humor, telling them, "If you don't think there is mental illness in your family, you haven't been to a family reunion lately." I shared what happened in my onset of mental illness, what had helped, and what my hopes were for the future. I told them that mental illness is a no-fault brain disease and yet also a spiritual battle. I told them that of all the medical providers who had worked with me, the most life-giving were the ones who went beyond the chemistry experiments of trying different medicines and lovingly invited me to choose life. Because they provided me with the truth that my life mattered, I found the courage to go on living. Now, almost three decades since my last psychiatric hospitalization in this very same hospital, the freedom from the chains of mental illness made me a kind of ambassador with a mission of diplomacy to break down barriers of stigma and fear.

The students listened with rapt attention to the stories my co-presenter and I told. They asked good questions. They clapped long and loudly at the closing of our presentation. Tap dancer Arthur Duncan once said, "Applause is like food for an entertainer. And thank you for that steak dinner you just laid on me."

I believe God gave each of us the gift of story to help us understand and love one another better. No one deserves to be told, "Your story doesn't matter." When our stories are evoked, when questions are asked of us with kindness and curiosity, something magical happens. We feel heard. It changes the story we tell ourselves. It opens the door to thinking, *Maybe I really am a person with a story of courage and dignity to tell. I'm gonna take a chance and see what happens when I tell my story.*

There was a time when my story came close to being silenced. In the summer of 1987, I was admitted into the University of Iowa Writer's Workshop for Poetry for a one-summer class led by poet Gerald

Stern. This was my goal for riding "the dog" across the country to Iowa City in the first place, and I should have been overjoyed and full of self-confidence. But my thinking was horribly distorted. I told myself that I was out of my league and that I could never be as talented as the other students. I couldn't really remember what my story was about. Most importantly, I forgot *who* my story was for. My story is to give glory to God. I had barely finished the workshop class when I tried to take my life. But I was a survivor of that suicide attempt and am a survivor in continuing to tell my story.

God doesn't waste anything. God used my perceived failure in not further pursuing the Writer's Workshop to show me how strong I am when I admit my weakness and rely on the strength of the spirit. It made me humble in a positive way, embracing my gifts for story-telling while acknowledging that other voices are equally creative and deserving to be heard. To this day, I continue to walk beside my fellow creatives for mutual encouragement and critique. I've been especially inspired by my friend and fellow writer, Marcia Murphy. You can read her inspiring writing on her web page: hopeforrecovery.com. Another dear sister in faith was Heidi Siemens Rhodes, who met with me and Marcia to workshop each other's writing. Tragically, she died of cancer on her 39th birthday in 2012.

Another insight from my brief time in the Writer's Workshop was that the audience I was writing for are persons needing to know that they are not alone in life's challenges. We're all in recovery from something. Our hearts are all in need of mending. Knowing that purpose helped me persist in writing. It was okay if I wasn't published in literary journals because that's not really my style. I am proud of my down-to-earth writing for faith publications. As my brain healed, my writing became clearer and more straightforward. I still use poetic imagery in my prose, but I hope it's not too hard to wrap your head around it.

And, almost miraculously, in 2005 to 2006, a University of Iowa Writers' Workshop student ran an outreach called *The Patient Voice Project* that matched persons in some kind of health recovery journey with writing tutors who were Writers' Workshop students. The tutors had a series of writing prompts and encouraged free-flowing responses to them. In 2006, they published a chapter book of participants' writing that included my poem, *She is Still Red*.

Another way I found my voice was in speaking to groups of people. I will always have a deep gratitude to a member of First Mennonite Church of Iowa City, Carol Enns, for calling forth gifts I didn't know I had for public speaking. In the early 1990s, she organized a worship service for Mental Illness Awareness Month and asked me to be a speaker. It felt like she had asked me to be a preacher, which was a little "scare-citing." I thought about it and said yes, though I would be pressed for time to prepare a talk as I was busy training for a 125-mile bicycle ride over two days to raise money for Multiple Sclerosis.

The weekend before the Sunday service, I went riding toward North Liberty, Iowa. I got separated from my friends and crashed my bike, tumbling head-first into gravel. I could barely crawl to my hands and knees and get up. Fortunately, my helmet protected my skull because my brain really didn't need more challenges. I walked up to a nearby farmhouse, and the kind homeowner drove my bicycle and me to the hospital. I needed stitches in my forehead and chin and had to have my knees and elbows bandaged up. I had two glorious shiner black eyes and bruises all over. Oh, and I broke a tooth and had a veneer placed by dentist Ann Connors, who remains a wonderful friend and supporter to this day. I ended up canceling the fundraising bike ride, but I kept my promise to give my testimony at the church service. I was the perfect image of a wounded healer. And I enjoyed it! I could feel the affirmation from the congregation deep in my bones.

After that boost to my confidence, I had the courage to accept other speaking engagements, some even paid gigs. I've spoken to Carol

Enns' Cornell College students studying Abnormal Psychology. I've talked to medical and Physician Assistant (PA) students on their psych rotation. One of the PA students who heard my talk went on to become my psych PA. I've given talks to Iowa State Prison employees who were being trained in intervention with prisoners facing mental illness challenges. I'm proudest of all for educating men and women in law enforcement about how it feels to be a person in a mental health crisis when police are called, as once happened to me in a suicidal crisis in the early 1990s. Knowledge is power, and hearing our stories gives law enforcement officers the power to intervene effectively and humanely.

It is not an exaggeration to say that "storytelling saves lives." It is the mission of the *This is My Brave* movement to empower individuals to put their names and faces on their true stories of recovery from mental illness and addiction. At *This is My Brave* performances, participants demonstrate courage in telling their stories through speeches, songs, poetry, dance, and visual arts—as many ways of expressing themselves as stories to be told. I performed at the Coralville Center for the Performing Arts in 2015 and again at the Englert Theater in Iowa City in 2017. You can watch my dramatic monologue, "On Being the Helen Keller of Schizophrenia," on my web page, www.margalea.com.

Psalm 107:2 says,

> *"Let the redeemed of the LORD tell their story*
> *—Those he redeemed from the hand of the*
> *foe."*

Eugene Peterson's *The Message* paraphrases the verse: "All you set free by God, tell the world." How can I keep from telling my story? I can't let fear hold me back, because love is stronger than fear. I can't let shame block my story because I've been forgiven, healed, and renewed. I can't let discouragement get in the way of telling my story because I get more encouraged whenever I tell of the obstacles I have overcome. I can't let my story be shouted down because I keep hearing God's still, small voice whispering in my ear, "You are my beloved."

Chapter 19

The Key of Remembering and Honoring Battles

I am writing this chapter on Memorial Day. I did something brave, today, something I'd been procrastinating. I received hard copies of my psychiatric medical records two weeks ago, but they just sat on the corner of my desk, daring me to read them. What if reading negative comments triggered trauma? What if reading about my revolving door hospitalizations made me feel ashamed and defeated? What if the doctors who considered me a hopeless case were right?

But the longer I waited to read my records, the more I was giving away the power of my own voice and story. I decided Memorial Day would be the perfect day to read them.

One of the ways I mark Memorial Day is to watch the public television program recorded live outdoors in Washington, D.C. In between musical performances, actors give dramatic monologues bringing to life the hellish experiences military veterans overcame. The stories tell of the loss of friends in combat, leading to sadness and sometimes guilt for escaping death. Their battles don't end when they come home from active duty. Many have had traumatic brain injuries and Post Traumatic Stress Disorder. As a Mennonite, I strive to be an advocate for peace. But my father fought during World War II in the South Pacific and I honor and respect him for his service. It was time to read these records and acknowledge my recovery battles with respect and self-compassion.

I opened the envelope and took out a thick stack of paper. The top document was a discharge summary dated November 19, 1984, at the end of a 14-day hospitalization. That was a long hospital stay for a young person trying to hold onto a full-time job as a hospital secretary. I remember trying to keep the hospitalization a secret from my parents, thinking they would be too worried about me. A law had recently passed in Iowa requiring staff doctors to ask patients to sign a release of information, allowing family to be informed of what was going on. After not communicating with my parents for a day and a half, I was asked to sign a release of information by a doctor who was kind enough to explain how important it was for my parents to be informed about my hospitalization. After I signed the release, my mother and father talked with me on the phone and told me how much they loved me. The discharge note doesn't mention my being asked to sign that release, but what a gracious mercy it was. Records say my discharge diagnosis was Bipolar Affective Disorder, depressed. I was sent home on lithium and Tegretol *"to better control affective episodes."*

The second hospitalization was July 4-10, 1985, following a Mellaril and alcohol overdose. The doctor commented:

> *"We discussed with the patient that her suicidal gestures in the past appeared to be more of a call for help. She agreed with this and entered into a discussion of a more appropriate method of seeking help."*

The third hospitalization was June 19-July 24, 1987, following a transfer from Med/Psych Unit following an overdose attempt with isopropyl alcohol; it mentions my having *"command hallucinations which became more troublesome, more derogatory, and suggesting self-harm."* It says I was found unconscious by friends (that would have been Marnetta) and taken to the hospital. That was my longest and most serious hospitalization and the closest I have ever come to death by suicide.

The note continues:

> *"Following her medical stabilization on the Med/Psych Unit, Ms. Warner was transferred to the Psychiatric Hospital where ECTs (Electric Shock Treatments) were begun. The patient had a dramatic response to her course of 6 ECTs. Since ECT #2, she has experienced a complete lack of auditory hallucinations."*

Most of that hospitalization is a blur, but I do have distinct memories of my parents flying urgently to Iowa and visiting me in the hospital. My mother brought me a tiny teddy bear clown with a colorful hat. She said it reminded her of my clown act personality, Parlay Voo, a character I named myself after being trained as a Christian clown. I also remember my dad brought me a ripe peach. They kept their visits short because I was still quite ill. It is puzzling to me that my discharge diagnosis was Bipolar Affective Disorder with mood congruent and incongruent psychotic features because it sure sounds more like schizophrenia to me. The note also says I was to be put on the waiting list to be seen by Psychiatric Nursing for counseling. That proved to be life changing because it connected me with Liz Schacht, ARNP, whose compassionate cognitive therapy helped me challenge distorted thinking and problem solve my challenges.

The fourth hospitalization was March 31 through April 1988. The discharge summary relates a grim story of something that happened during that hospitalization:

> *"She went out on a pass and went to the Sheriff's office and applied*

for a gun permit. The Sheriff's office was later contacted and the permit was terminated."

The note further relates:

"She on occasion attended work from the hospital but it was noted that she was somewhat irritable at times and could throw temper tantrums. Over the past three days she has been more calm but without any fluctuation in her mood. Her problems were discussed with her employer who describes that she usually does an adequate job and for the past couple of days she has done an adequate job."

They must have talked to my wonderful, compassionate boss, Dr. Phil Schmid. What a miracle it was that I kept my job!

This time the discharge diagnosis was "schizoaffective disorder." Nardil and Tegretol were discontinued and I was restarted on 900 mg. of Lithium BID. Why still no antipsychotics?

The fifth discharge summary is dated February 19-23, 1989, but it states that it was my 12th psychiatric admission. The University of Iowa Hospital records don't include my Maryland hospitalizations or my hospitalizations at Mercy Hospital of Iowa City. That number captures the relentless revolving door experience of hospitalization after hospitalization.

The note relates:

"She has been hearing voices that told her to kill herself and that she drank half a bottle of Kahlua alcohol in a suicide attempt. She displayed paranoid ideation in that she felt her counseling sessions with Liz Schacht were taped and played to her fellow workers at the VA Hospital."

My discharge diagnosis was finally changed to chronic schizophrenia with secondary depression versus schizoaffective disorder. It mentions the possibility of underlying temporal lobe epilepsy, and so I was sent home on Tegretol and Haldol, an older antipsychotic.

Later that year, July 10-27, a sixth hospitalization.

> *"She admitted to thought broadcasting and auditory hallucinations. She exhibited paranoid ideation—convinced her phone is tapped at home and that others could hear her thoughts through a device in her head. Loxitane (an antipsychotic) was started on 7/12. The patient expressed decreased auditory hallucinations. Discharge medications were Lithobid, Cogentin, Retin A Gel (the lithium caused years of terrible acne), Colace and Tetracycline."*

I feel so much compassion for my then-29-year-old self. My brain was so broken! I needed to find a way to manage an illness that was so unmanageable. I needed to LIVE with this illness instead of dying from it. I wish I could have told younger me, *"You can beat this, but you have to take responsibility for your own recovery."*

I credit myself for staying out of the hospital from 1989 until 1992. The note from the seventh hospitalization, January 16-25, relates,

> *"She continues to hear voices gossiping through the heating vent. She heard a male voice telling her she would be better off dead and suggesting that she stand on the railroad bridge over the river."*

Discharge diagnosis was schizoaffective disorder, depressive type.

The next note is from the eighth hospitalization, this one in the Mental Health Clinical Research Center from February 3-24, 1993. The last paragraphs of the CRC note are intriguing to me:

"In terms of our staffing for Margalea, there was a consensus diagnosis of paranoid schizophrenia at the moderately high confidence level. However, there were many of us who knew Margalea well enough to confirm a secondary diagnosis of borderline personality traits. Although she probably doesn't fulfill criteria for the disorder, she has the impulsivity, affective instability, manipulative fear of abandonment, dependency, and multiple suicidal ideation and gestures characteristic of a borderline.

In reference to her medication management, we feel that Margalea does not have significant affective component that warrants Lithium treatment. We feel this should be discontinued and it will take care of many secondary side effects she has been experiencing for quite some time. In addition, Margalea had questioned the indication for Clozapine. Because she responded so well to Loxitane, we do not feel that Clozapine would be indicated at this time. We suggest she be continued on the Loxitane therapy."

It's hard to read those judgmental words. I don't believe I have borderline personality disorder, but I have friends who do, and they have benefitted from Nancee Blum and her STEPPS and STAIRWAYS programs. We could all use help challenging distorted thinking and processing our emotions. But I agree with the wisdom of stopping lithium. It wasn't helping me mentally, and it was causing years of disfiguring acne, diabetes insipidus, and thyroid problems.

There was a ninth hospitalization from February 24 to March 3. Again, the diagnosis was Chronic Paranoid Schizophrenia. Discharged on Loxitane. Another hospitalization July 9-14, discharged to the Clinical Research Center for another research study, this one comparing Olanzapine and Haldol. I sensed I was on Haldol because I recognized the side effects of it from being on it in the early 1980s. I was discharged from the inpatient part of the study considered stable.

I took a deep breath before turning to a tenth discharge summary dated August 16 to September 8 because I knew this was the next to final hospitalization, a life-changing hospitalization.

> *"The patient was admitted because of a suicide attempt of jumping into the river after hearing voices telling her to do so. At the time of the admission, she had been enrolled in the Lilly protocol, but this was discontinued due to her exacerbation of her illness, which required hospitalization. The Clozapine protocol was initiated on 8/19/93. The dose was gradually increased until 8/28/93, when the patient became febrile. The dose was then held at 200 mg until the fevers resolved and was then increased gradually beginning on 8/2/93. By 9/5, she was at 300 mg q d, 100 mg q am and 200 mg q hs. After the reinstitution of the increased dosage, the patient tolerated the medication without any further fevers.*
>
> *After the patient denied further experiences with auditory hallucinations and suicidal ideation, she was gradually allowed out on pass. She was quite active and apparently did quite well with her passes to church, out with friends, and also on an almost daily basis to attend work near the end of her hospital stay. Condition on Discharge: The patient was tolerating her Clozaril dosage well and was denying any auditory hallucinations or any suicidal ideation."*

The summary is signed by Delwyn Miller, M.D., Staff Psychiatrist.

Reading that makes me pump my fists and yell, "Yay! Yay! Yay"

There was one more ordeal ahead of me. My outpatient psychiatrist took me off Clozapine, even though I was tolerating it well, and switched me to Risperdal, which he thought would be equally effective without the immune system risk. It wasn't as effective. I struggled to sleep at night. The voices became menacing. Also, I had breast lactation. To add to the stress I was experiencing, I had started a new job as secretary for the Physical Therapy Graduate Program. I used

PCs instead of Apple computers in a front office with little privacy, answering dozens of flashing button phone lines. My eleventh and last hospitalization was from June 9 to June 29, 1995. Clozapine was restarted, but I was still overwhelmed. Even while hospitalized, I had another suicide attempt while on pass, jumping into the Iowa River, rescued by fishermen who called the fire department. One of the firefighters who responded knew me from Faith UCC, and he let other church members know to pray for me.

> "She was dysphoric and sad for a while but eventually her mood improved. She was able to go out again. She was continued on Clozaril. She was discharged without suicidal ideation. She feels good about herself and about going to work again. She feels she is ready to leave."

And leave is exactly what I did! And for 29 years, I have not returned.

Reviewing my mental health story in the words of the psychiatric professionals who treated me has challenged me to accept the past that I cannot change and the courage to focus on the positive life progress I have made. At some point, those doctors may come across my published book. I wonder what they will make of my story. I hope they can give me some grace for coping with my no-fault brain disorder and credit for strength in persisting in my recovery. It's my story and I claim the last word of my story—and that word is *Victory*.

Chapter 20

Let Tears Come

I admire my parents so much for lovingly welcoming me into their lives as a baby when Mom was 39 and Dad was 44. I'm amazed how they found the resources of time, energy, and patience to raise me and that they did it with so much love and grace. The only hard part about their ages was that I lost them when I was younger. It was a privilege to walk them Home. I am so grateful that I did not take my life and avoided breaking my parents' hearts with the hardest kind of grief there is. And even more wonderfully, they got to see me heal and thrive before they passed away. Loving much meant grieving much, but I was able to grieve without shame or regrets. I let tears come in a healthy way when they passed on and my life on this earth continued.

I found a note from my mother that I put in my jewelry box to always treasure. It isn't dated but was likely around Christmas, 1996. In beautiful cursive writing, she wrote:

> *Dearest Margalea, I can't begin to tell you how much it means to me to have you here. If we had no celebration, if we*

had no gifts for each other, it would make no difference. The important thing is for you to be here. I don't mean to take away from the celebration. I don't mean to diminish the gifts. Both were important. The gifts were lovely. But the important thing for me was that you are here. Love, Mom.

Just two years later, I lost my mom when she was only 77. That seemed young because her mother lived to age 90 and other women in her family lived long lives. She suffered on a respirator in a nursing home for the last seven months of her life. It seemed so unfair. She started smoking in the 1940s because her brother told her a menthol cigarette would be just the thing to soothe a sore throat. Both of them were deceived by advertising that cigarettes weren't bad for your health and that "More doctors smoke Camels." She tried hard to stop and was finally able to do so with meditation. She hadn't touched a cigarette for ten years before she developed emphysema and had to be hospitalized in August 1997.

The doctors asked my brother and me if we wanted her to have a tracheotomy so that she could have a respirator put into her throat. Both of us were bewildered with grief and couldn't decide that for her. We asked the doctors to ask her. On an alphabet board, she spelled out "y-e-s." Her will to live was that strong. After the procedure, she was transferred to a nursing home in Virginia that specialized in respirator care.

My brother was her main caregiver because he lived in Arlington, Virginia. My father, who was then her ex-husband, visited weekly. Once he brought her a Scrabble game and asked her if she wanted to play Scrabble. She looked excited to play so he started opening the board. But then she shook her head no. It was too much of a struggle for her. That broke Dad's heart and he said to me over the phone, "She has no quality of life."

I flew from Iowa to see her in September of 1997 and stayed in my father's home in Rockville, Maryland. I relied on friends to help me get to the nursing home as it was over an hour's drive in heavy traffic and not near a Metro subway stop. When I walked into Mom's room, I was struck by how bright blue her eyes were, magnified by her eyeglass lenses.

"Hi, Mom, it's me," I said and slid my arm around her shoulder in a sideways hug.

She couldn't speak much because of the respirator but she reached for an alphabet board and patiently spelled a greeting.

"Hi, Honey!"

The effort of typing those short two words seemed to exhaust her.

Then a few more words: "I think I'm going to spit up."

I called the nurse and she brought a basin that Mom retched into.

We sat together and watched some television. Mom was a devoted watcher of Wheel of Fortune. I still delight in watching that show. I remember how good she was at solving the puzzles and how frustrated she would be when she shouted out the right answer and the contestant didn't listen. These days, I bounce on my little trampoline watching it and I jump with joy right along with the winners. Mom was the winner of living with the puzzle of suffering and persisting in love.

I wish I could have had more days with her in the nursing home, but a week later, I had to get back to work. David did a wonderful job keeping me connected to Mom, reading her my letters and cards, and arranging for me to make phone calls to her. He let me know that her health was getting more and more frail. Mom's two best friends, Marcia Brewington and Carol Fitch, visited her around Christmas. They were terribly distressed by how near death she seemed and they urged me to come see her immediately. Knowing my finances were tight, they asked Seekers Community of Church of the Saviour to donate some money to cover my airfare. I bought a ticket right away. Dad had the idea of asking his sister Catherine if we could stay with her in Virginia to be closer to the nursing home. Aunt Catherine kindly opened her home to us. I flew into National Airport on December 31 and was able to wish Mom a happy New Year the next morning.

I prayed in the shower that week, and sometimes cried, because it was so hard to watch Mom struggle to breathe, be given just a little oxygen but denied more because she would stop breathing on her own if they gave her too much. It was as if she were drowning.

A week later, Marcia Brewington took me out to breakfast at McDonald's and then to the nursing home for one last visit before I had to fly home. Dad met us there and we all gathered around Mom's bed.

"I love you, Mom," I said. "I bet you love me too. Do you?"

I was teasing, mostly wanting to coax her into speaking.

She had a twinkle in her eye, and she breathed out, "Nooooo!"

We all knew she was joking by the big grin on her face and the laughter she coughed out.

"What about Marcie (Mom's nickname for Marcia)? Do you love her?"

"Noooo!"

"What about Dad?"

"Nooo!"

"We love you too, Mom!"

We took turns reaching down and embracing her.

I went back to Iowa and prayed for her to be given a merciful release from the ordeal of the respirator. At three in the morning on March 24, 1998, I was awoken by a phone call from the nursing home.

The caller spoke in a flat monotone, "Your mother has expired." She didn't even soften it with "I'm sorry."

"We don't have a morgue," she continued. "What plans have you made for the body?"

"I-I don't know," I stammered. "Have you called my brother?"

"Yes, but he didn't answer."

I told her I would call him myself. After five rings, I reached him. I was glad I got to give him the news more gently than she did. He said he would call the nursing home for us.

Then there was nothing to do but to try to go back to sleep. I pressed my face into my pillow and tried to muffle my sobs. I felt my big tiger-striped cat, Taz, step onto my pillow. Then he licked my cheek with his rough tongue. It was as if he were a mama cat and I a kitten! And I knew that though I had lost my mother, I had not lost God's love.

I was 37. I was determined to go on living in a way that would make Mom proud. Mom had already seen me stay out of the hospital for almost three years. She had witnessed me getting to my goal weight at Weight Watchers.

As I write this chapter, daylilies are in bloom. It reminds me of how Mom would pick me up after school and ask me, "Do you want to go on a ride?" She always kept county maps in her glove compartment; she liked to explore new roads into rural areas. We'd drive past masses of orange and yellow daylilies. She lived her life one daylily at a time. I strive to do the same.

About a year after we lost our mother, my brother David wrote me a letter saying,

> *Yes, dear sister, I feel her presence most truly, with the least distortion, when practicing paying attention to my is-ness through three relaxed breaths at a time, and/or asking the questions: What made Her/you/me? What is/are/you/I made of? What put Her/You/I here? Focusing on the effort to asks the questions, not some small answer created by my mind, is when I feel her intentions for us—still fresh from her Being—to see what and who we really are and all the sour baggage of fears and doubts will dissolve away into the dust of illusion.*

He signed the letter, "Rhooghur, Dave." Rhooghur was a word our mother created as a family endearment based on the French word for Mom's favorite color, "rouge." It was more powerful than the sometimes cliché love.

There were some further life milestones that I got to share with my dad. On October 10, 1999, my birthday fell on a Sunday when First Mennonite Church was having a retreat at our church camp. My pastors, Bob and Mag, had insisted that my dad, who was in Iowa visiting me, and I come on the retreat. We might not have gone otherwise, but since they insisted and gave us a ride, we came. We stayed in the lodge Saturday night and Sunday morning attended worship. I could tell my father was bursting to tell the congregation, "Today is Margalea's 40th birthday."

During children's church time, a church member read the children a book called *The Quiltmaker's Gift*. Then I was asked to come forward. Pastor Mag put into my arms an enormous, wrapped package that felt squishy. I tore away the paper and revealed a beautiful friendship quilt. Church members had each made unique blocks with messages for me and alternating blocks were stylized cats with button eyes. I was so moved, I cried, and Dad was right beside me, crying too. I have the quilt hanging on my living room wall and it is like a birthday card that I open every day.

In May 2002, Dad got to be with me at a banquet for Goodwill Industries where I received the Emily Helms Award. In honor of the daughter of Charles and Leila Helms, the Emily Helms Award is given annually to a person who demonstrates character in facing a disability. My schizophrenia doesn't seem like a disability, and it didn't keep me from working, but it still was a life challenge, and it's good to be affirmed for facing it with character and a sense of humor. My friends in NAMI had nominated me for it. It was a big deal. Right before the banquet, Dad pinned a pink carnation on my jacket. My friend Mary, whose clown name is Mrs. Hinkey Dink, came in costume. Pastor Mag gave the invocation. Many of my peers were also honored with awards for their accomplishments, and there was thunderous applause for each recipient, though mine seemed the loudest to me. I got to give my acceptance speech at the very end of the ceremonies. Dad was so proud that he was laughing and crying at the same time.

Later that week, Dad and I flew to Vancouver, British Columbia, to take a train ride through the Canadian Rockies. This was something my dad had wanted to do for decades after his aunt had made a similar trip in the 1950s. I'm so glad we did it when we did.

In June of 2007, my dad's health deteriorated as he battled prostate cancer. He was hospitalized in Maryland. I battled his insurance company and the health care system to get him well enough to come live in Iowa close to me. I ended up flying there to advocate for him in person. Finally, the day came when we were riding with Dad's spiritual director, Jerry Parr, and his wife to National Airport to fly to Iowa. Jerry turned from the front seat to the back seat and put an El Salvadoran embroidered minister's stole around Dad's shoulders.

"Phil," Jerry said, "we are commissioning you to be a shepherd and a pastor of the Iowa City nursing home where you are going. They need your gifts for laughter and friendship. Do you accept this assignment?"

Dad said, "Yes." More tears! We are a family of criers. He came to Iowa with me, strengthened by a sense of purpose.

Once in the Iowa nursing home, the doctors said Dad had perhaps six months to live and admitted him to hospice care. Iowa City Hospice helped put life into Dad's days when they couldn't add days to his life. He discovered the hospice chaplain had done her internship at Church of the Saviour and they had long, deep conversations. He adored the nurses and the nurse's aides. He played Scrabble with hospice volunteers and talked them into bringing him coolers full of non-alcoholic beer and sharp cheddar cheese.

First Mennonite folks helped us, too. Dad was matched with Stephen's minister, Lynn Lehman. Lynn was an elementary school teacher. Each week, he brought a few different fifth-grade students to visit Dad and hear stories of all Dad had lived through, including the Great Depression and serving in the Navy in the South Pacific during World War II. The kids laughed at all Dad's corny "dad jokes."

One of Dad's favorite jokes went like this:

A man went into a bar for happy hour. He heard a chorus of tiny voices saying, "What a nice suit you are wearing." He couldn't tell where they were coming from. Again, the voices chirped, "And that bow tie you're wearing is so classy." And then he heard, "You've got the brightest blue eyes." Bewildered, the man asked the bartender who was saying such kind things.

"It's the peanuts," the bartender said. "They're complimentary."

When Dad passed away quietly the morning of January 1, 2008, at age 92, I could hear voices all around me saying, "You are my beloved daughter." I was bewildered by where the loving words came from—

from inside of me. Yet, I was also surrounded by supportive friends who seemed to agree with the voices identifying me as *beloved daughter*.

Words of comfort also came at Dad's Iowa City memorial service. Lynn Lehman gave one of the eulogies, saying what an amazing person Dad was. In between stories, Lynn blew his nose into a big purple handkerchief and wiped away tears. I loved him for doing that.

We played two recorded songs during the service that were favorites of Dad: "It's a Small World" and "You Are My Sunshine." Sitting in the front of the church in a pew next to my spiritual director, Dorothy, I got the giggles, and Dorothy giggled right along with me. Dad would have been happy that we did that. Marty Stoltzfus played Dad's favorite Dixieland Jazz song, "When the Saints Go Marching In." I did a little dance in my seat.

Dad's spirit seemed close a year and a half later when I celebrated my 50th birthday. I threw a party for myself that was kitty-themed. I asked guests to bring donations for the Witty Kitties special needs cat shelter. I had a cake made with a photo transfer of me and my cat Taz. Dad was one of the few men Taz trusted and would allow to pet him. I found a picture in Dad's wallet of me with Taz in my arms. I also had a friend make me a "kitty litter" cake with pudding and cookie crumbs and melted tootsie rolls spelling out happy birthday. Some people were probably horrified and found it in poor taste, but it tasted good and it got all eaten up.

Another thing that made me feel closer to Dad was taking classes in the Wu style of tai chi led by Joseph Wyse at First Mennonite Church's fellowship hall, starting in January 2012. Watching Joseph do the slow, meditative movements made it look so easy but doing it myself was way more challenging. Practicing tai chi required practicing self-compassion and not giving up. It reminded me of Dad playing golf and the joy he found in swinging the club and tapping the ball from the green into the cup. He played up to age 91 despite loss of arm strength. If he could persist in joyfully moving his body even without being a perfect golfer, I could persist at tai chi. I took the beginning level class twice in 2012 and the advanced level class two other years. Joseph named me "The Triumphant Tai Chi Tortoise" for keeping up my practice and slowly improving.

Dad was a faithful letter writer. He mostly typed his letters, which was helpful because his handwriting got increasingly illegible. One was from Easter 2007, written on rainbow-hued stationary:

> After the storm of winter and despair, truly Easter shouts, He lives. He lives in rainbows and in kittens, robins and cherry blossoms. O friend, rejoice. He is risen! We are reborn! Alleluia. Let's sing and dance. We live because he lives. Amen! Love, Dad.

The last immediate family goodbye was my half-brother, David Kingsley Crombie. His middle name, Kingsly, is related to my mother's family history of a Scottish king granting us a "lea" of land. So, men in our family, like my uncle, had middle names of "Kingsley," while women, like my grandmother, were named "Lea." My nickname and writing name is Margalea, which is short for Margaret Lea. Most of my life, I heard my brother called David, but after Mom passed away, my brother preferred to be called Dave. And I was most surprised to hear our cousins call him "Dicky" and hearing that was short for "Dicky Bird." It seemed a little too playful and childish for a 70-year-old.

On January 7, 2016, I received a shocking phone call at work from an Arlington, Virginia, detective, Rose Munizza. My brother's body was found by his landlord, who had entered when he hadn't seen David for a week. Finding my brother's decayed body collapsed on the sofa, the landlord was bewildered and didn't know how to reach my brother's family, so he contacted the police. That was how this detective was assigned to the case. She couldn't find an address book but found my return address on a birthday card with a caption: "To my dear brother" that I'd sent him in May of 2015—by some miracle, he had kept it in the envelope! She guessed that I was his sister, even though we had different last names from different fathers. She Googled my name, found some of my writing, and was able to contact me. What a God-thing that she was able to put those clues together! My heartache lessened when she told me that they had sent the body to David's family doctor, who determined the cause of death was likely a stroke. The doctor identified his body, so I didn't have to identify him from photographs of his decayed body, which would have been gruesome. My brother was only 70 years old when he died.

My grief at losing my brother was complicated. As a recovering alcoholic, my brother was suspicious that my taking psychiatric medications was like relying on street drugs or alcohol. It was hard to explain to him that the meds supported my brain health so that I could think clearly and process the feelings and emotions I was living with more skillfully. In a way, NAMI was my AA.

My brother could be moody and angry, but he seemed to find greater peace toward the end of his life. He told me how helpful it was to do Buddhist sitting meditation. He liked to reminisce about our mom and our growing-up years in Arlington, VA. He sent me a clipping from the Washington Post with a story about a mother tiger with her two kittens that had just been born at the National Zoo. He wrote underneath the picture of the tiger family, "You, me, and Mom." I keep that picture on my bulletin board just inside my front door and fresh flowers on the shelf below it.

Rereading my brother's letters made me cherish him even more. He was so protective of me. In one letter, he wrote:

Thank you so much for the Valentine cookies. I eat one

or two or... with coffee when I get home. Hope you remember to wash out all teethy wounds immediately that you acquire when playing with Taz. Washing them out may be sufficient, they could become septic if unattended. Iodine/Lysol also good. Mom stopped taking her vitamins and supplements at some point. Can I send you some? How about some of her curtains?

Over the years, David generously mailed me things from our mom, always expertly wrapped and packaged. He sent a hinged wooden box with a doll passed down from our great-grandmother, and a wardrobe of clothes our mom had sewn for the doll. He sent a shelf built by our grandfather with a secret compartment into which he carefully enclosed a crystal vase of our mother's that she called Baby because it was shaped like a pregnant woman's belly. He loved hearing about my cats, and when I sent him pictures of them, he would enlarge photo prints of them. He ended phone calls saying, "Take care of the kitty."

With the help of my beloved cousins Allison and Carolyn, I went through my brother's belongings in his apartment the week after he passed away. A family treasure I had help getting home to Iowa was our family dining room table, which had legs that could be twisted off and a folded top. Marnetta and Jerry brought it in the trunk of their car when they came to Iowa the following June. David had refinished it and protected it with a shiny, clear coating.

I also found a warm gray sweater in my brother's cupboard, which I immediately put on to stay warm during the very cold January day my cousins and I spent going in and out of his apartment. It felt like a hug from him.

I was also pleased to find that my brother had kept a little clay bird statue I once sent him. It reminded me of the song, "His eye is on the sparrow, and I know he watches me." Of course, my pet cats always had eyes on the sparrow in a more menacing way.

The most precious final gift from my brother was almost lost. We found a heavy black trash bag on the bottom of his closet. We opened it and gasped at what we found. It was full of black and white family photographs. Many were taken by our grandfather, who had his own photo-developing black room. I think David put them in the trash bag, planning to take them to the park and burn them. He told me he was going to do that to keep them from falling into the hands of strangers when he died. I'm so grateful he didn't get around to doing that and that family found and kept them. My cousin Carolyn added them to an electronic family album and shared them on our family Facebook page.

What have I learned from these losses? I've learned that I can lose the lives of people dear to me without losing my wholeness and joy. I have integrated their love into my body and spirit. Sometimes, I feel lonely, but when the sadness comes, I reach out to these friends I've been blessed to know, and they invite me into their family. I haven't lost my family of origin because nothing can separate us from the love of God. I got to walk them Home, and that's all that matters.

Chapter 21

Standing Ovation for a Heroic Mom

The applause after the performance of *Unfinished* ballet couldn't have been louder if the whole audience had had cymbals for hands. Dance Professor Eloy Barragan and his dance students came forward for an exuberant curtain call, holding hands and bowing in unison. Afterwards, I went backstage to toss them flowers and give each one a big hug.

But there was another individual who deserved applause just as loud, a woman named June Judge. She's the mother of Michael Judge, who, with me, is listed in the program as a source of inspiration for the ballet. June is my hero because of the courage she demonstrated in raising and nurturing five children: Steve, John, David, Katherine, and Michael. Her two oldest sons, Steve and John, lived with schizophrenia, the latter taking his life at age 21. She lost Steve to a heart attack when he was just 54. I remember getting the news about his death in an email, just a week after June, Steve, and I had attended an educational program at NAMI Johnson County where a presenter said patients with schizophrenia can expect to die 15-25 years younger than the general population, without considering the likelihood of death by suicide, because the illness and medicines used to treat it impact physical health. June donated from Steve's memorial fund to the newly opened NAMI Peer Support Center in Iowa City called R Place. The donation covered the center's rent for a year.

June's son, David, was diagnosed with a disease that attacks the kidneys in his 30s, and he received a donor kidney from his youngest brother, Michael, in his 40s. The kidney lasted for fourteen years. The transplant kidney "wore out" in 2016, and David had to start dialysis. I would run into David as he walked up the hill to the hospital for dialysis treatments while I was walking on my lunch hour. He still had a spring in his step and was upbeat and friendly. When Covid hit, kidney transplants were put on hold, and by the time they restarted transplant surgeries, he was not considered eligible for a transplant because of his overall health condition. To the end, he was a lover of plants and nature. You could even call him a plant whisperer. June and her family lost David to kidney failure in 2023 at the tragically young age of 60.

How June survived these terrible losses and kept her strong spirit is hard for me to comprehend. I think it had to be a combination of faith, love, and a stubborn will to live for the sake of her family and because of her commitment to a campaign advocating for serious mental illness.

While only two of June's children were diagnosed with serious mental illness, she made sure all her children were exposed to leaders in the field of psychiatry to gain awareness that mental illness was a no-fault brain disease. She pushed back against doctors who blamed families for causing mental illness, especially the Freudian sexism toward "schizophrenogenic" mothers. Her daughter Katherine became a social worker, and her son Michael a journalist.

June didn't limit her advocacy to only her family. The group now known as National Alliance on Mental Illness (NAMI) came to be because of June and other visionaries like her. In 1977, families in

Madison, Wisconsin, whom I like to call "The NAMI mommies," gathered around a kitchen table to discuss the challenges of raising children with serious mental illness. When June heard about their initiative, she helped found NAMI in the state of Iowa as well as affiliates in the state.

I graduated from high school in 1977, the same year NAMI was launched. My mental illness was waiting in the wings to walk onto the stage when I turned 22. I didn't discover NAMI until decades later. How I wish my own mother could have met June. The two of them would have had a wonderful conversation full of humor and hope. What stories they could have told each other!

I first met June in 1995 at a NAMI meeting, not long after my last psychiatric hospitalization. I credit her for urging me to faithfully continue taking the psychiatric medicine that worked so well for me, Clozapine. She told me what a huge difference the medicine made in the quality of life of her son, Steve, and her daughter-in-law, Diane.

June and I started giving talks to church groups together. We were a good match for that—hers from the family perspective, mine from the perspective of the individual with the illness. We both leaned on our faith for strength without being preachy and fiercely opposed religious stigma toward "the mentally ill." Neither of us thought prayer alone could cure mental illness. We shared a sense of humor born of the belief that stigma is ridiculous and laughter is contagious.

In early September 2024, I met with June to ask her more about her story and to bring her some cheer and affirmation. My friend Linda Hug was the perfect person to join me. Linda's family name is spelled and pronounced just like the embrace, and they live up to the warm friendship implied in their name. Linda's parents, Dan and Phyllis Hug, helped launch NAMI of Johnson County, Iowa. Linda has family members with mental health challenges, and she lives in recovery from depression. The Hugs and the Judges have long been friends and supporters of each other. June and I attended the memorial service for Linda's oldest sibling, Carolyn, in July 2024; it was a bittersweet reunion.

In 2024, Linda named her NAMI Walk team "NAMI needs a Hug." I joined her team and invited June and her family to join us. Our team was strengthened by Michael, Masae, and Maximillian, whose family nickname is "3M." I was the lead individual fundraiser, raising $6,000, and our team was the second-place fundraiser, raising over $9,000.

Linda and I met June outside her senior living community, where she eagerly awaited our visit. Before I could give her the flowers I'd brought her, she gave me a big hug, so I kind of hit her on the back with them. She gave Linda an equally warm hug. With the Hugs and the Warners properly hugged by June, we went inside to the dining room.

After we were seated, a resident friend of June's (actually, all the residents are her friends) approached our table, looking a little lost, and said, "I need to sit down somewhere."

"Sit with us," June replied, gesturing to the chair beside her. June introduced us to the woman and said matter-of-factly, "She has aphasia."

The woman sat down with us. While her speech and memory seemed challenged, she was mindful enough of the present moment to compliment me on my bright orange blouse and Linda for her "Childless Cat Lady" t-shirt. She was especially delighted by the flowers we had brought for June. June put them in the water carafe on our table when the retirement home staff refused to give us something to use as a vase. I enjoyed that moment. It was so typical of June —practical and spunky.

After lunch, we went to June's apartment to meet privately. The three of us sat close together to watch the ballet video on my phone. June oohed over the beauty of the young dancers as the movement began. She cringed when the chorus of dancers bullied the lead dancer, especially when they seemed to be ripping at her clothing, or perhaps her very guts.

When the dancers made stiff, jerky movements in unison, June said, "That's TD!" TD, or tardive dyskinesia, is a syndrome of involuntary movements caused by some psychiatric medicines, especially the older antipsychotics. There are medicines to treat TD but they have side effects too.

When the "unfinished symphony" came to an abrupt stop, so did the dancers, and the stage lights were darkened. Moments later, Eloy and the dancers came forward for a curtain call.

"Bravo!" June exclaimed. "Bravo!"

I asked June if she would like me to read from the ballet program next, and she said yes.

I showed her the cover, which featured a photograph of the lead dancer in a simple white dress leaping in the air, almost flying. Then I read, "Dance 2 *UNFINISHED*: Inspiration: Margalea Warner and Michael Judge."

As I've said before, Michael is June's youngest son, and his friendship with University of Iowa dance professor Eloy Barragan inspired the ballet. Michael introduced me to Eloy, who interviewed me about my recovery journey with schizophrenia. Eloy wrote:

> "I was first inspired to choreograph "Unfinished" when I read my dear friend Michael Judge's interview with world-renowned Dr. E. Fuller Torrey, author of Surviving Schizophrenia. Michael's family story—his two older brothers, Steve and John, suffered terribly from schizophrenia, the latter taking his own life at 21—moved me greatly, as did his family's perseverance and determination to advocate for the estimated 14.2 million others in the U.S. who suffer

from serious mental illnesses such as schizophrenia, bipolar disorder, and depression."

"Yes! Yes!" June exclaimed. "He got it right."

I asked June for more details about how serious mental illness impacted her family but tried not to pry in ways that might trigger emotions about family tragedy. I knew from talking to her daughter, Katherine, that Steve was a 21-year-old cadet in the Air Force Academy when he became very ill with encephalitis. He recovered from encephalitis but soon displayed symptoms of psychosis and was diagnosed with schizophrenia. His next younger brother, John, also experienced schizophrenia when he turned 21. The two brothers were very close. The whole family was heartbroken when, after five months of brutal psychosis, John took his life, leaving behind twin daughters who were almost two years old. My visit to June came close to the anniversary of his death, and I was so sad for her revisiting the tragic loss.

June said, "I knew I couldn't stay silent about mental illness when Steve got sick. I needed answers. I wasn't about to give up on my family. There had to be a better way to treat mental illness than just locking people up, or worse, sending them out, without treatment or support, to be homeless."

I asked June about E. Fuller Torrey's influence on her family. Dr Torrey is an American psychiatrist born in 1937 who experienced his sister being ill with schizophrenia. His love for his sister led him to approach mental illness as a neuroscience, not caused by personal weakness or bad parenting. He wrote a groundbreaking book titled *Surviving Schizophrenia: A Family Manual*. Since its first publication in 1983, *Surviving Schizophrenia* has become the standard reference book on the disease that has helped thousands of patients, their families, and mental health professionals alike.

June told me how her daughter, Katherine, told her to come quickly to the television to hear Phil Donahue interviewing "a psychiatrist who doesn't blame moms and families for causing schizophrenia."

June contacted Dr. Torrey and invited him to speak to the NAMI chapter she had started in Iowa. Unfortunately, bad weather forced him to cancel his visit, but June went ahead with the gathering anyway, starting an important dialogue in Iowa about how mental illness needs to be discussed openly instead of hidden in shame.

In the summer of 1983, Dr. Torrey came to Waterloo, and June insisted that her son, Michael, go and hear his talk. Michael was 16 years old and tormented by the suffering of his older brothers, his heroes.

June said, "I was losing Michael, and I just had to get him to hear Dr. Torrey."

Michael told me how much it helped him to hear from Dr. Torrey, saying,

> "He made me realize, for the first time, that schizophrenia was a disease of the brain like one can have kidney disease or diabetes or cancer. It was no one's fault, least of all, my family's fault or my brothers' fault. It freed me to love them and see what they suffered was an illness, not a character flaw. He saved me. As did my mother! And sister!"

I continued reading the program aloud to June:

> "I chose Schubert's Unfinished Symphony to accompany the dance because schizophrenia strikes most people in young adulthood, leaving their lives "unfinished" in so many tragic ways. I have worked with so many young dancers who struggled bravely with mental illness. I dedicated Unfinished to all of them, those who are

with us and those who aren't—and every family ever touched by brain disorders like schizophrenia, bipolar disorder, and depression."

Linda Hug commented, "Yay, he mentioned depression too! That's an equally serious mental illness."

I asked June what gave her hope to go on after so much loss.

> "What gives me hope is how my family loves each other and how they care for each other. I first became a Special Education teacher because I was concerned about learning disabilities for one of my children. I've always been a teacher. I believe if you educate people, they will change and have understanding and compassion for our folks instead of reacting with hate and stigma."

I love that June calls people with mental illness "our folks" and "our people." I remember years ago her commenting that she liked it when NAMI changed its name from "National Alliance for the Mentally Ill" to "National Alliance on Mental Illness." She said at the time, "It's stigmatizing to label individuals with mental illness the mentally ill as if they were all alike and defined by only their illness. Put the person first. They are individuals living with mental illness."

We moved into June's bedroom to watch videos on her VHS player—yes, she still has a VHS player. First, she played a television clip about the Compeer program. Compeer is an international program based on the simple but brilliant idea that wellness begins with friendship. The Program matches adults who are living with mental illness with community-trained volunteers to create intentional friendships to reduce isolation and loneliness. June was responsible for launching three chapters of Compeer in Iowa.

I can testify from experience that my friendship with my Compeer matches (I've had three of them) has mutually benefited both sides of the match and made our lives more meaningful and joyful. I also served on the Compeer of Johnson County board for 20 years before retiring in 2024.

Then June played a video of a research study tracking responses to Clozapine over weeks, months, and years of treatment. June's son Steve and her daughter-in-law Diane had a huge improvement in quality of life by being treated with the medicine.

In the video, patients are interviewed before and after taking Clozapine. The difference is night and day. In "before" interviews, the patients ramble in word salads and express paranoia about terrifying hallucinations. They appear somewhat disheveled. I joked that they had much better haircuts in the "after" interviews. Linda said, "They are better groomed." Their speech became more directed and easier to understand. They seemed much calmer and less frightened. The longer the interval after starting the medicine, the better they seemed to be doing. These individuals were able to return to the life that their mental illness interrupted, including holding paying jobs, living independently, and being involved in the community.

After we finished watching June's videos, June had something else to show us. She lifted a framed award off the shelf and read aloud from it. It was an award given to June in 2020 called the E. Fuller Torrey Advocate Award. (That same year, Dr. Torrey got a national award for being an exemplary psychiatrist.) It honored June for her years of persistence and ferocity in advocacy and education. How wonderful that life should come full circle that way, June being affirmed for how she took Dr. Torrey's life-saving research to help her family and families around the country. June quipped, "Maybe we need more doctors who have a family member with mental illness."

The day after our visit with June, June phoned me and said how wonderful it was to get together. I don't know why I had the audacity to ask June, "Can I be adopted into your family?" I am the only one left in my immediate family, having lost my mother in 1998, my father in 2008, and my half-brother in 2016. June took me seriously!

She checked first with her daughter Katherine, then with her son Michael, and even with her daughter-in-law Masae. The vote was unanimous to include me! We even set a date to eat supper together and then watch the television show Sixty Minutes.

June turned 88 on September 23, 2024. With the loving support of her family, she is facing the challenges of aging with courage and optimism.

Bravo, dear June! You are my hero for choosing dance over despair. You have helped me and all "our people" find keys to joy and recovery.

Chapter 22

The Key of Celebrating with Keys

Here's the story behind literal collection of keys, which I've collected and named for concepts behind my recovery. It was inspired by friendships with two sisters in faith, love, and laughter: Sherry Gordon and Becky Kessler. We met while attending Faith United Church of Christ in Iowa City. I also connected with Sherry at a Saturday morning "breakfast club" sponsored by a visiting counselor group we were both members of.

Sherry is my peer in recovery from mental illness, and she is also a person in recovery from substance abuse. She has stayed clean and sober since 1990, starting the year she moved from Ohio to Iowa City. She calls Iowa her "dry state." Her twelve-step groups, Alcoholics Anonymous and Narcotics Anonymous, celebrate milestones of abstinence with daily chips and yearly medallions. Our friend Becky was so moved when she heard Sherry's recovery story that she wanted to throw Sherry a party and invite others to join in celebrating Sherry's ongoing victory.

Becky invented a most creative ritual: a non-alcoholic drink contest with Sherry as judge. Guests pre-prepare the most delicious non-alcoholic drink they can imagine. Usually, only six to eight drinks are entered in the competition because the gatherings are small, and some guests are intimidated about creating a winning drink. Sherry jokes about accepting bribes to give prizes, but no one believes she would be an unjust judge. As an added precaution, Sherry is blindfolded before the tasting ceremony. After tying a colorful scarf around Sherry's head, Becky places each drink into Sherry's hand, telling her which number she is tasting. Sherry inhales the "bouquet" before sipping a mouthful and swishing it around.

"Ooh, drink number one is delicious," Sherry says. "So is drink number two."

Spoiler alert: She never says anything negative about any of the drinks.

Finally, it's time for her to rank the drinks, starting with the lowest ranking (but still wonderful, amazing, and delicious) and concluding with—drumroll—the first-ranking drink.

Then the blindfold comes off and the names of the drink creators are revealed. Sherry goes on and on with superlatives about how delicious all the drinks were and what wonderful people we all are for coming to her party. Then the winners (we all are winners!) get to pick a prize from the gift table of items Becky has saved up over the year, including books, perfumes, scarves, and practical things like holders for corn on the cob.

Sherry's party was an inspiration for all of us. For me, especially, it made me long to celebrate my mental health victories. My equivalent of years of sobriety was years without psychiatric hospitalizations. There's no shame in being hospitalized when you are in a mental health crisis, but staying well in the community is something to celebrate.

By June of 2012, I had been free of hospitalizations for seventeen years. This was also the year I started taking tai chi lessons from Joseph Wyse in the First Mennonite fellowship hall.

In Wu tai chi, there is a concept called "the seventy percent principle." In a literal sense, practitioners are taught not to push their bodies beyond seventy percent of what is comfortable and balanced. It's the opposite of no pain, no gain. Joseph promised that if we respected our seventy percent, our seventy percent would grow over time. In the years since my last hospital stay, I've respected my seventy percent by not exceeding my limits. I take my psychiatric medications and supplements because I know that chaos follows if I don't. I keep appointments with my psychiatric providers because I value their empathy, instruction, and wisdom. I choose routines like early bedtime and early morning meditation. I benefited from a visiting counselor support group and matured in my daily life skills. I kept my job as a secretary at University Hospitals, where my supervisor, Claudia Bishop, affirmed me as a valuable employee, as did the doctors I worked for. I am not disabled by my illness; I am differently abled. My seventy percent capacity for recovery has grown large indeed.

So, it was time for a party! Since one of the most disturbing parts of being hospitalized was having heavy locked doors slam shut behind me, keys were the theme of the celebration. Becky graciously offered to host my "Key Party" at her home, saying I could invite whoever I wanted. Of course, the first guest I invited was Sherry! Ahead of the party, I asked each guest to bring me a random key they might have around the house. I got a variety of keys—car keys and house keys, antique skeleton keys, and even some actual University Hospital keys that a friend who worked there had captured after the locks were changed.

I didn't know what I would do with the keys when I got them. As keys came to me, I put them in a metal cookie tin. I carried the tin on the bus, causing strangers to stare at the rattling noise they made. I closed my eyes and touched them, one by one, pretending I was Helen Keller making sense of them. I fingered them like prayer beads.

By the night of the party, I had chosen seventeen of the keys to keep, one for each year of life free of hospitalizations and suicide attempts. I named each one based on concepts, tools, skills, coping techniques, healthy habits, and plain stubborn determination, which got me there. After a delicious meal and a drum roll, I told my story, key by key. My friends' applause was louder than the noise the keys made knocking around in the cookie tin. In the following years, I displayed the keys in a shadow box that overflowed into a second shadow box. As of June 2024, I have earned 29 keys.

I do have moments when I feel locked out of my recovery. I hear voices muttering that I am an imposter. They snarl, "Who do you think you are?"

That's when I turn to my friends for a spare key. They say, "Margalea, you know who you are. You are God's beloved. You are a wonderful friend. We love hearing your stories. You've got this because God's got you."

Then, I hold each key in my palm, feeling the weight and coolness of the metal, seeing how it shines in the light. I pick the best key to open the next locked door.

Chapter 23

The Why Behind My Keys

In this final chapter of *Choosing Dance Over Despair*, I want to name the keys I've collected and explain why I chose them.

My keys begin with basic first steps: Key 1 is *right meds* and Key 2 is *talking therapy*. While I don't necessarily rank my keys in order of importance, these two are essential. They are connected. When I first had the onset of psychosis, I had an issue called anosognosia, meaning my brain wouldn't recognize that my brain chemistry was playing tricks on me. Cognitive therapy helped me overcome my distorted thinking and accept the need for treatment. I say *right* meds because I went through a decades-long chemistry experiment before I found the right one for me and committed to taking it consistently. I built a habit of setting up my medicine boxes weekly. I set an alarm for 8:30 p.m. to take my psych medications, which make me sleepy, half an hour ahead of going to bed at 9. I guard my sleep habits. I'm an unapologetic party pooper when it comes to asking to leave early from late-night gatherings.

The medicine that worked for me is an antipsychotic called Clozapine. Just as my house keys don't open your front door, my medication may not unlock your mental illness or the mental illness of someone you care about. But I do want to make you aware of Clozapine. Clozapine was discovered in 1958 and is now considered the "gold standard" therapy for treatment-resistant schizophrenia. It is an "atypical" antipsychotic, meaning, in contrast to typical antipsychotics, it does not produce significant extrapyramidal side effects, does not elevate prolactin levels, and does not induce tardive dyskinesia after long-term use. Sadly, Clozapine wasn't used in the United States until 1990. I wish I could have started taking it sooner.

I must add a word of caution about Clozapine. In rare cases, it can lower immune response and make patients vulnerable to infection. I have a friend and peer who almost died of pneumonia because his white count went below zero. However, doctors who prescribe the medicine are cautious to do frequent lab work checking to ensure immune markers remain normal; they stop the medicine immediately if the lab results are abnormal. Please do good research and be well informed about whether this is the right way to treat serious mental illness in yourself or your loved one.

Key 3 is *family*. I had unconditionally loving parents. They supported me through the worst times of my life. They understood my mental illness was not caused by poor parenting. They understood I had not caused my mental illness by bad character. They helped me learn from experience and make better choices.

In my early thirties, I called my mother to ask if I could return to live with her.

She wisely said no.

Since then, I have heard the advocacy slogan that people with mental illness need not just housing but housing that heals. Whenever I am asked to give a talk to a NAMI Family to Family class, I jump at the opportunity. I love telling my story in ways that bring them understanding and hope. Since I have survived all my immediate family, I treasure friends who have become my family of choice.

Key 4 is *Compeer* and *All True Friends*. The root meaning of compeer is equal friend. I have been blessed by equal friends, especially peers in mental illness recovery. But the Compeer program has added to my community of support by matching me with trained community volunteers. Matches are made based on mutual interests, such as hobbies, age, and location. My Compeer friend Della McGrath and I get together weekly to do things like go out for meals or ice cream, go for rides in the country, shop, and run errands. Yesterday, we had a wonderful time at the Compeer Fall Social. I was on the Board of Compeer of Johnson County before I retired, but Compeer remains a heart song that I will always work to support.

Key 5 is *Let Tears Come*. It's healthy to cry when life is difficult, especially when grieving the losses of family, friends, and pets. Some grief is more complicated than others. One of the most hurtful things that was said when I was less than a year into grieving the death of my father was, "You should get your s--- together." I did try to get my life together, but conflicting emotions came in unpredictable waves. Grace and healing came from therapists, pastors, and friends. Lament released does eventually lose its power over us. Psalm 30:5 says,

> *"For his anger lasts only a moment, but his*
> *favor lasts a lifetime; weeping may stay for*
> *the night, but rejoicing comes in the*
> *morning."*

Key 6 is *The Dignity of Work*, which applies more broadly than paid work and is sometimes as small as doing the dishes. My true life's work started with retirement, giving me a chance to be productive in writing and being published. Retirement has been re-inspirement.

Keys relating to psychosis include Key 7—*Tell the Voices Not Now* and Key 8—*Challenge Distorted Thinking*. I have not experienced hearing voices or special messages for a long time, probably thanks to effective medical treatment. But that gives me all the more sense of purpose to support my peers by attending a NAMI support group called *Hearing Voices, Special Messages*. We are part of a club that nobody wants to join. To each other, we are intimate friends and peers.

I admire the group's facilitator, T, who lives so courageously with paranoid schizophrenia. He says he fully believes signals are being broadcast into his brain, but he chooses to act as if the real, trust-worthy humans in his life know better. Some members of the group have command hallucinations urging them to break into houses or do self-destructive things. When members are too tormented by the voices to say *no* to them, they tell the voices *not now*. The voices don't need to know that later never comes. J once told her voices, "I don't pull into oncoming traffic on Wednesdays." When one of us was chal-lenged by religious delusions, D asked, "What do you know to be true about the character of God? If God is all-loving, how could God hate us and want us to die?"

Keys related to spirituality include Key 9—*Prayer* and Key 10—*Choose Life*. I've been blessed by faith communities that did not have a distorted view of mental illness as sin or demon possession. Some of my peers have not been as lucky. I've given talks to religious groups, making me feel churches can be receptive to education.

I have reached out to my church for prayers for healing, including being anointed with oil. I wasn't immediately cured, but it was a step in the right direction. In the mid-1990s, I commissioned a healing-themed friendship quilt. Eight friends embroidered quilt blocks using line drawings from the *Good News Bible* as a template. I made the ninth block using a drawing from the Bible story about how friends lowered their friend through a hole they made in the roof so he could get to Jesus. My friends acted just as loving as those friends did, carrying me to help when I didn't have the strength to walk to it by myself. It can take so much strength and courage to choose life. I do so only by the grace of God.

One key makes me giggle: It's attached to a fingernail clipper; how weird is that? One of my friends who wanted to contribute to my key collection didn't have a key he could give me. So, he reached into his pocket and pulled out a fingernail clipper. I thought it over. Some people do have fingernail clippers on their key chains. And the fingernail file that twists out from inside could pick a lock in a pinch. So, I named Key 11 *Think Outside the Box*. I urge doctors and researchers to find unconventional and creative solutions to treat mental illness. Of course, I don't want my cat to think outside the litter box!

Two keys relate to physical health: Key 12—*Walking* and Key 13—*Healthy Eating*. In my teens and twenties, I stayed slender almost effortlessly. But in my thirties, various challenges made me gain almost 30 pounds. Side effects of psychiatric medicine caused some of the weight gain. Some medications made me so thirsty that I drank a lot of "pop"—even diet pop wasn't good for me. A lifelong non-driver (I got a D on the road in Drivers Ed and brought it up to a C with class work), I have always gotten exercise by walking, but I did too much sitting at work and home. At age 38, three years past my last psychiatric hospitalization, I was ready to make a life-changing decision: I joined Weight Watchers. There was a Weight Watchers meeting place near me, right next to a Dairy Queen restaurant. I sometimes wondered if they were in collusion!

As soon as I came in the door, I knew I was in a safe place. This was a place of acceptance and encouragement. I learned so much about healthy eating and exercise, but the most important thing I learned was that I am a person of dignity and worth and that I deserve a healthy body.

The weight came off slowly, which was good because it gave me a lot of practice with healthy habits. How did I reach my goal weight and keep it off since 1998? I started drinking more water and unsweetened iced tea. I began bringing snacks when I was away from home so I wouldn't be tempted by fast food. I took long, romantic walks through the produce aisle and bulked up meals with fruits and vegetables. I ate real food instead of frozen diet meals. I used more spices like basil and oregano and less salt.

Weight Watchers uses the word "activity" instead of exercise so that people who don't consider themselves athletic can be encouraged to think that anything that gets them out of their chair is beneficial. I asked myself why I stopped doing exercise that was so much fun as a child. I purchased a little trampoline and bounced to *Wheel of Fortune*. When the players win and jump for joy, so do I. I walked the hospital halls during my lunch hour, aiming for 10,000 steps a day. I was so proud for walking in a 10K walk, and I got a Weight Watchers charm for doing so. Later, I added strength training at home with dumbbells and sit-ups.

If I had to choose just one Weight Watchers tool that helped me be successful, it would be tracking what and how much I ate. Weight Watchers food plans have come and gone, but the habit of tracking has remained constant. My Weight Watchers app told me this morning that I am on an 801-day streak of recording food and exercise. I probably would have been credited a longer streak if the Weight Watchers app hadn't crashed at some point. Another helpful practice is to say a prayer of grace before meals, even when I am eating alone.

I think it is a false dichotomy to separate mental health from physical health. It's hard to have one without the other.

One key has whiskers; Key 14 is *Kitties and Critters*. My pets have included parakeets and finches, one goldfish, and five cats: Who Me,

Taz, Conroy Chester Charles the Third, Millie, and Helen of Toy. These critters have brought me company and comfort.

Key 15 is *Tai Chi and the 70% principle,* which contains the wisdom not to push yourself—body or spirit—past 70% ease and comfort. It was my experience that though I learned tai chi slowly and awkwardly, the more I respected 70%, the more my 70% grew. That was how my teacher named me *The Triumphant Tai Chi Tortoise.*

Simple keys that say what they mean in one short word include Keys 16, *Faith;* 17, *Laughter;* and 18, *Hugs.*

Key 19 is *The Key to the Quiet Room.* It's the actual monster-sized, heavy antique key to the room where I was once isolated and held in restraints.

Key 20 is *This is My Brave,* based on storytelling theater performances in 2015 and 2017. You can watch my dramatic monologue, *On Being the Helen Keller of Schizophrenia,* on my writer's web page, Margalea.com

Key 21 is *Massage,* a form of self-care that I have benefited from for years, helping ease anxiety and bring me peace in the present moment.

Key 22 is a pledge to say: *I wish I were in Paris* instead of *I wish I were dead.*

Key 23 is *Music,* an image for the wisdom that sometimes our minds are off key and need piano tuning. The key I chose for that title was given to me by John Bixler, and it is the key that opens a piano keyboard cover.

Key 24 celebrates advocacy, both personal and community-wide: *Ask for what you need.* I chose it based on a travel adventure in 2019 when I got stuck in the Denver airport overnight. I got up the courage to approach a fierce security guard and ask her for help finding a safe place to sleep. She responded to me warmly and helped me with everything I needed, including a paramedic to take my blood pressure, a sandwich from McDonald's (I said I didn't need fries, and she said, "Yes, you do."), getting me a boarding pass for the next morning, and giving me a blanket to sleep beneath on the airport chapel floor.

Key 25, *Gratitude*, calls forth the best in all that surrounds you. I chose this key title in 2020 in the middle of the Covid lockdown. Keeping a daily "three good things a day" journal helped me hang on. Anabaptist World magazine challenged writers to reflect on the theme, Joy to the World, and they published my essay, *The Joy of Gratitude*, in their Christmas 2020 issue.

Key 26: In 2021, I named the key *Persistence*. That year, the Mars Rover was named "Percy." I have a refrigerator magnet that says, "Never, never, never give up."

Key 27 is *Dancing in the Dark*, chosen the year of the *Unfinished* ballet. I ask myself, *What if instead of running from schizophrenia, we danced with it?*

In 2023, I added Key 28, *Sabbath*. I define sabbath as create, rest, repeat. One of the blessings of retirement is that I live with Sabbath rhythms. An example: as I've been working on this book manuscript, I have set a timer for 30 minutes to write like crazy; when the timer goes off, I get up and go for a walk.

Key 29 is *The Gift of Story*, my key for this year, 2024. I believe God gives each of us a story so that by sharing our stories, we can grow in love and compassion for one another. Why did I write this book telling my story? Because the story kept calling me to tell it. I've always dreamed of telling my story in book form. I didn't want to reach the end of my life without making that dream come true.

I also tell my story to pay forward the hope I got from my peers in mental health recovery, especially my NAMI "Peer to Peer" mentors. I tell my story to encourage a young homeless man named Nathan, newly diagnosed with schizophrenia, that recovery is possible. I tell my story to help families recognize they didn't cause the no-fault brain disease of mental illness in their family members. I tell my story because I believe everyone is on a recovery journey of some kind. I want to walk beside the whole world in getting better. I tell my story to mend broken minds.

I can finally tell my story as a published book because I had a story coach named Marcy Pusey who wouldn't let me put off completing the draft by teaching myself to play the banjo or any other silly thing my brain invented to procrastinate writing.

I gave myself the gift of finishing this book when it was good enough instead of when it was perfect because perfect never happens. Only God is perfect, and I'm not God. My job is to be a good steward of the story God gave me, and that is enough.

I have been pregnant with this book for a year and nine months. The due date has arrived. I have endured fierce labor pains, but they are almost forgotten as I witness the birth of my story. I can't wait to hold my published book in my hands.

I choose to dance over despair. Will you join me?